Deliciously Balanced Asian Meals in 30 Minutes or Less

WOK ON

Ching-He Huang

For my mom and dad, my No.1 fans.

Ching-He Huang is an Emmy-nominated TV chef and cookery author. Born in Taipei, Taiwan, her culinary ethos is to use fresh, organic, ethically sourced ingredients to create modern dishes that fuse Chinese tradition with innovation and are accessible for home cooks. Her immensely popular TV series include *Chinese Food Made Easy*, *Chinese Food in Minutes*, *Exploring China* and *Ching's Amazing Asia*. She has also been a regular guest chef on *Saturday Kitchen* and *This Morning*.

Ching has written eight bestselling cookbooks: *Stir Crazy*, *Eat Clean: Wok Yourself to Health*, *Exploring China*, *Ching's Fast Food*, *Everyday Easy Chinese*, *Ching's Chinese Food in Minutes*, *Chinese Food Made Easy* and *China Modern*. She is also the creator of The Lotus Wok—a wok with a dynamic nano-silica coating for high performance cooking. Ching divides her time between the UK, the US, and Asia.

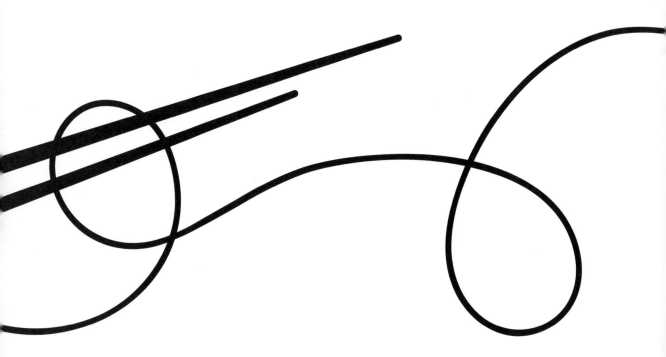

Deliciously Balanced Asian Meals in 30 Minutes or Less

WOK ON

Ching-He Huang

Kyle Books

An Hachette UK Company
www.hachette.co.uk

First published in Great Britain in 2019 by
Kyle Books, an imprint of Kyle Cathie Ltd
Carmelite House
50 Victoria Embankment
London EC4Y 0DZ
www.kylebooks.co.uk

This edition published in 2019

ISBN: 978 0 85783 712 7

Distributed in the US by Hachette Book Group, 1290
Avenue of the Americas, 4th and 5th Floors, New
York, NY 10104

Distributed in Canada by Canadian Manda Group,
664 Annette St., Toronto, Ontario, Canada M6S 2C8

Publisher: Joanna Copestick
Editorial Director: Judith Hannam
Editorial Assistant: Isabel Gonzalez-Prendergast
Design: Caroline Clark
Photography: Tamin Jones
Food styling: Aya Nishimura
Props styling: Wei Tang
Production: Gemma John

A Cataloguing in Publication record for this title is
available from the British Library.

Printed and bound in China

10 9 8 7 6 5 4 3 2 1

INTRODUCTION

Ni hao! Hello!

Thank you so much for picking up *Wok On!* I very much hope it will inspire you to take up a wok and get cooking. I know it's not always easy to stay motivated and make meals from scratch, but I've been doing this a while, and I promise you, home-wokked dishes using fresh ingredients are always going to be better for your health and deliver more in terms of live enzymes and micro-nutrients than supermarket-prepared food. The trick is to make it fun, and soon you'll be on your wokstar journey —I apologize now in advance for the wok jokes! There'll be plenty! #Wokscooking!

Wok on follows on from my *Stir Crazy* cookbook, which was all about stir fries. *Wok On* likewise includes stir-fried dishes, but also focuses on the techniques you may not have considered when using your wok—steaming, shallow-frying, braising, and deep-frying. My aim is to show you that armed with this one-pan wonder, you can make a huge variety of meals.

I have included new, occasionally crazy (though in a good way!) recipes such as My Mom's Sriracha Ketchup Shrimp, Kirakuya Fireball, Dirty Hoisin Cranberry Kimchi Pork & Hot Cheese Sandwich, Golden Sesame Shrimp Balls, Hoisin Duck & Strawberry Wok-Fried Crispy Wonton Tacos and Macanese-style Codfish and Potato Balls, which might raise a few eyebrows, but I promise they are all utterly delicious.

If you are after ease and speed, I have plenty of delicious options, including some reworked takeout favorites. Designed with busy wokkers like you in mind, they are simple enough for everyday cooking, and super healthy too. They include dishes such as Shrimp Ban Mein, Wok Fried Beef in Chili Sauce, Spicy Smoked Bacon Broccoli, failproof Crabmeat Corn Soup and General Tso's Chicken Wings, as well as Chinese-in-taste comfort foods such as Taiwanese-style Seafood Pancake, Ching's Fish Ball Noodle Soup, Drunken Scallops with Samphire, Soy Bean Sprout Cilantro Cheung Fun Rolls, Chicken with Ginger Choi Sum and Goji Berries, Sichuan Bacon, and Leek Wok-Fry.

And since there is a growing demand for vegan food (my husband is vegan), I have included many recipes that are vegan. In fact, Chinese vegetarian food is mostly vegan (if you omit eggs) as we use virtually no dairy in our cuisine, and instead rely on tofu, mushrooms and other vegetables, and nuts. So if you are looking to eat more vegetables, most of the meat dishes can be made vegan with a few simple substitutes. Some of my favorites are Sichuan Chile Tomato Mock Chicken, Saucy Mushroom and Ginger Tofu, Sichuan Spicy Salt and Pepper Mock Duck, Veggie Ground "Pork" with French Beans, Vietnamese Style Golden Tofu Noodle Salad, Vegan Pho and Thai Green Sweet Potato Curry.

If you love to entertain, and are looking for variety and versatile dishes, then this book is for you too. I love to entertain and often double up the recipes for a Chinese-style buffet for family and friends. You can have something in the steamer, in the pot, in the oven or rice cooker, and then a couple of woks on the go! My Ching's Macanese Minchi is great for a Sunday brunch, Black Pepper Mock Duck and Basil Shen Jian Bao Dumplings are great as party food, Oxtail and Turnip Noodle Soup is easy to do for a large crowd for dinner, Golden Macanese Cod, Crispy "Family Snapper" with Black Bean Sauce, Miso Honey Ribs, Vegan Crispy Dumplings, Addictive Crispy "Seaweed", Braised Hong Sao Pork, Beef & Mushroom Beijing Whole-Wheat Pancakes, Beef and Pea Wontons, and Pearly Beef Balls are great family friendly dim sum dishes. My dumpling and dim sum recipes can also be frozen, so all you need to do is boil, steam, or wok-fry when you need them.

And if, like me, you're a fan of rice dishes, I have plenty to satisfy your taste-buds, from Black Pepper Bacon Pineapple Fried Rice, Smoked Salmon and Egg Fried Rice to Japanese Rice Omelet (Omu-Raisu), to Pork and Kimchi Water Chestnut Fried Rice, and Black Pepper Duck and Kale Wokked Rice; there is something for everyone!

I've also discovered a love of fusing dishes and in particular, draw quite a bit of inspiration from Macao, a small region just off the South China Sea, with its fusing Portuguese, African, Indian, and Chinese influences. In terms of rediscovery,

perhaps my favorite "seasoning" or flavor pairing in *Wok On* is Oyster sauce (mushroom sauce if you are vegan) and black pepper—the result is an addictive and powerful flavor combination! A little of the seasoning goes a long way. I don't like to over-season my food and am always careful not to go overboard on the sodium, preferring to use tamari or low-sodium light soy sauce where possible. Which brings me to ingredients. I choose organic and higher welfare whenever possible—it's much better for both you and the planet.

So, this book is designed for you to make it your own—to make substitutions and add vegetables you prefer. Whether it's a saucy dish, or a dry noodle fry that you are after, whether you're a meat or veggie vegan lover, a novice or a total wokstar, I hope the dishes will help you increase your kitchen repertoire, and bring some balance to your eating.

So enough chatting, let's get wokking!

Wok on my friends, and I sincerely wish you happy eating always!

Love,

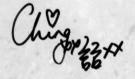

WHY USE A WOK?

Why use a wok?

The ultimate kitchen implement, this 2,000-year-old magical cooking pot is a way of life all over Asia. Perfect for sautéing, braising, frying, and steaming, it can be a lifesaver on busy days.

How do I go about choosing a wok?

My grandmother used to cook in a cast-iron wok, and they are the best, but they are extremely heavy, and it can be difficult to toss the food or maneuver them away from the stove top when the heat gets too hot.

Most Chinese chefs use unseasoned carbon steel woks, but these require a lot of love and care, or they rust. Nonstick varieties are available, but are not ideal as the coating comes off with time. Some carbon steel woks have a flat, wide base more like a saucepan, which is not a traditional wok shape, so look for ones with deep sides (to allow you to toss the food) and a small center (to concentrate the heat). Traditional woks are round-bottomed, but these require a wok ring set over your hob, which is another added piece of equipment, and not ideal for the modern home, especially induction stove tops.

Stainless steel woks need to be seasoned with coatings of apple cider vinegar, each coating evaporated to give a clear, thin, nonstick layer. They are particularly good if you are into healthy eating, but don't retain heat as well as carbon steel, and sometimes have uneven heat spots, which means food can stick.

Aluminum woks are inexpensive, but they can rust and warp, and are not as good at either conducting or retaining heat as carbon steel woks.

Whatever wok you have, I always say it's best to use it and not waste it. When it's on its last legs and you need a replacement, please do seek out my Lotus Wok. I designed it for people who want a better wok experience. It is inexpensive and is made from carbon steel so that it heats quickly, plus it has a natural, "nonstick"-type, nano-silica coating (made from sand-blasted crystals). It is a medium gauge, so not too heavy, yet not flimsy. It's also scratch-resistant, so you can use metal utensils on it, and hydrophobic, which means it repels water, giving your veggies that crisp finish, and oleophilic, which means it allows just enough oil to coat the surface of the wok. It is a clever wok that just gets better with time—I have used mine for over three years now and it is still going strong. It comes with a wooden spatula, a glass lid, and a stainless steel steamer rack. You can purchase it on Amazon.co.uk. For more information check out www.chinghehuang.com.

Now you have a wok, what's the first step?

If you don't need to season your new wok, you can go right ahead and start cooking—just use a damp sponge and a little soapy water to wash off any industrial oil, dust, or dirt, rinse, then place it on the heat to dry. If you need to season your wok, go to my online video at www.youtube.com/user/chinghehuang, which shows you how.

The "Breath of the Wok"

Home wok cooking differs from restaurant wok cooking as the latter has wok burners that can reach 1200°F (far higher than the 350°F that the average domestic stove can achieve), but the one thing that differentiates a good stir-fry from a bad one is the "breath of the wok", a term used to describe the *wok-hei*—the "smoky flavor" that comes from a good flame-wokked dish, and the all-important balance of *xiang, se, wei* (the aroma, color and taste of the overall dish). Wok chefs in restaurants maneuver and operate a gas lever by the side of their legs at the same time as they toss the wok and flick it towards the flames so they lick the sides of the wok, injecting wok smoke into the dish. This is why I have so much respect for wok chefs—they have no fear of the flames, which can sometimes be over six and a half feet high. They inject the "breath of the wok" into the dish, as well as sauté, sear, deep-fry, shallow-fry, steam and braise, all in this one cooking vessel, and have the eye-to-hand-to-leg body coordination (wok dance as I often refer to it) to time the addition of each ingredient perfectly. Cooking on such high heat means that if you are one second out, your vegetables lose their shine or crispness, and is why perfect stir-frying is so hard to master. Consistent results take practice, timing, skill, and unwavering focus. However, this doesn't mean that you can't still get those smoky delicious results from wokking at home! I have some tips to help you.

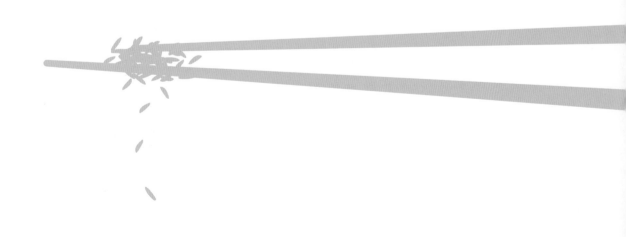

WOKKING TECHNIQUES

STIR-FRYING

This is perhaps the most classic use for a wok —a little bit of oil and lots of stirring will ensure that ingredients keep their crunch, and take on a delicious smoky flavor. For stir-frying, there are ways to help you get it as perfect as possible.

Preparation is king!

Ensure all your ingredients are prepped beforehand, and are as close to the wok as possible to save you time, and arm yourself with the freshest ingredients. If ingredients are substandard, you will be able to tell, because vegetables will not look fresh or bright, and once stir-fried, they will go limp very quickly. When it's "wok on", there is no time to do anything —least of all, to stop and chop!

The right oils

An odorless, flavorless oil that has a high smoke point, such as peanut oil, canola oil, or coconut oil, is best—it gives a neutral base on which to create your layers of flavor, yet is able to withstand high temperatures. Toasted sesame oil is really only used for seasoning.

What level of heat should I go for?

It's important to get your wok really hot before adding anything, so that you see a little smoke rising off the surface. At that point it's time to quickly add the oil, which will heat up instantly. Heating the wok first means the heat is evenly distributed over the entire surface. Once you add ingredients to it, the temperature in the wok starts to fall, but keep the ingredients moving to prevent them burning, or take the wok away from the heat source. If you are really worried about the flame, then heat the wok over a medium-high heat, and work your way up to maximum heat over the course of several stir-fries where practice becomes perfect.

Size and shape matters

Whenever you add several ingredients to the wok at the same time—for example, aromatics such as garlic, ginger, chiles and small pieces of onion, or different types of vegetables, such as shredded cabbage, carrot, and onions—it's important they are all a similar size, as this will ensure they cook in the same amount of time.

It's important, too, to consider the size of the main protein ingredient in relation to the rest of the ingredients. For example, if you are wokking beef slices, then make sure the vegetables are cut in slices too, so that the dish looks balanced. How you cut the ingredients is very important. If you slice on a deep diagonal, it exposes more surface area for cooking and it can also make ingredients go that much further. For example, wafer-thin, square-ish slices can be achieved by slicing across the grain of a cut of beef. Vegetables can be prepared in the same way, so a carrot can be sliced into round coins, or into long oval pieces if sliced on the diagonal. Play with the shapes and have fun!

Balance the aromatics—the awesome foursome!

I like to use a combination of garlic, ginger, and chiles—what I call The Holy Trinity—but now I sometimes add scallions to the mix too. Holy Trinity was so last year—now it's all about the Awesome Foursome! I have been accused of adding garlic, ginger and chiles in almost all my dishes, but this is because I try to inject their healthful, antibacterial properties into my cooking as much as possible, so that I am getting the maximum healthful nutrients in any one meal. But it is entirely up to you, and you can vary what you add to suit your likes and mood of course.

"Compartment" cooking

Compartmentalize your ingredients—group aromatics together, also the vegetables, and seasonings. Think of your protein and treat it separately—what flavors are you trying to achieve? Finally, think of your garnishes and ways to inject some freshness into the dish at the end. So break the recipe down. Sometimes, the dish looks like a long list of ingredients, but actually most are pantry ingredients and garnishes. So, the dishes are not as long or as difficult as they may first "appear"—after all—appearances are deceptive!

STEAMING

Food cooked in this way is super healthy! You can use a bamboo steamer and set this on a wok, or now stainless steel or bamboo racks can be set on top of a wok and all you have to do is pop the lid on. Both are relatively inexpensive. Bamboo steamers are versatile in that you can pile a few compartments on top of each other, so you can steam multiple dishes at once, and while steaming, they also give off a light bamboo fragrance. The stainless steel rack is good as it lasts a lot longer. Here are a few things to note before you wok steam!

Make sure the wok is stable

If you have a flat-bottomed wok, this will be fine, but if you have a round bottomed one, then invest in a wok stand as well, as you don't want to risk spilling over hot water and steam. Safety first!

How much water do I fill the wok with?

Fill the wok half-full with boiling water, and place the bamboo steamer on the top, making sure the base of the steamer does not touch the water. Depending on the recipe, either place the food to be steamed on a heatproof plate, bowl, or shallow bowl, that fits in the steamer, or on parchment paper, or on bits of food (for example, dumplings can be set on top of a small slice of carrot for function and presentation purposes). Put the lid on, and steam. If necessary, top up the wok with more boiling water as the food cooks. The trick is to make sure the bamboo steamer or rack you are using is stable, fits comfortably and securely within the wok, and there is minimal room for steam to escape. And so the size of the steamer and how it fits across the wok is important; the key is to find one that is big enough to steam a large amount, and fits snugly across the wok. You can pile up to 3 bamboo steamers high, any more and you may need a more powerful burner to create enough steam to reach the highest part of the steamer.

Hot steam

Before you attempt to take off the lid of the steamer, just take care and make sure you turn the burner off first. Gently lift the lid away from you, so the hot steam wafts away from you, and you don't burn your arms.

DEEP-FRYING

Deep-frying gets a bad rap as it's deemed an unhealthy way of cooking. Of course it isn't as healthy as a virtuous steamed dish, but much more sinful than a stir-fry, however, deep frying as a technique is not as bad as you might think. If the food is dropped into hot enough oil, the outside edges are sealed at high temperatures and the latent heat would continue to cook the food, and not allow any further oil to be absorbed into the food.

So the most important tip (apart from having a stable and secure wok—please refer to my wok stand tip in the stir-fry section), is to make sure the oil is at the correct temperature. For best results, invest in a good deep-frying thermometer and follow the recommended temperature in my recipes. If the oil is not hot enough, the food will take longer to cook, and the result will be greasy food. If the temperature is too high, the food will burn on the outside, and not cook through on the inside. If you don't have a thermometer, I would use the ginger or bread test, so add a cube of bread or small piece of ginger, and if it turns golden brown in 15 seconds, the oil is at 350°F, or thereabouts.

When you are ready to fry, use a slotted spoon or a Chinese "spider"—a web-like mesh scooper; both would work well as a strainer. Use it to lift fried foods out of the wok—helping to drain as much oil as possible in the process—then place the food onto a plate lined with paper towels.

The "spiders" are available from Chinese supermarkets and they come in various sizes; the handles are often made from bamboo.

When you start deep—frying, make sure the wok is stable, do not overfill the with oil (it should never be more than half full so there will be less chance of it bubbling, and food spilling over), make sure the food you are frying is not wet as it will spit in the hot oil, don't re-use the oil if you can help it—fresh oil will give fresher results. Use large tongs, or long bamboo chopsticks to help turn the food if necessary, and don't use plastic utensils as they will melt.

Ideally serve the dish immediately after cooking, as it will start to lose its crunch and crispness. However, if necessary, keep the food hot in a preheated oven before serving.

BRAISING

There are a few recipes that first require a quick 20-minute braise. After that, you can either wok-fry and brown the meats, then add some stock and the seasonings for a quick saucy or brothy dish. The results are fabulous in a wok because the deep sides allow you to add as much liquid as you want, and at the end of the cooking process if you want to add vegetables or noodles, the wok has enough room to allow you to do that, for an easy one-pot dish. The same rules apply as with all wokking or cooking, make sure the wok is stable on the stove.

BOILING

The wok with its deep sides is great for boiling—especially for soup broths, and works just like a pot, allowing you to contain a lot of food and liquid in it—so you can boil to your heart's content!

SMOKING

Smoking is not a technique I use in any of the recipes in *Wok On*, but it can be useful to smoke a small piece of fish or duck. The trick is to set the wok on hot fruitwood chips, Jasmine rice, or whatever flavor you like, and place the stainless steel rack on top. Then place the meat or fish, or tofu on a heatproof plate on top of the rack, close the lid, turn the heat to very low, and let the smoking ingredients at the base gently burn to create smoke for your dish.

EQUIPMENT

In my recipes, I like to keep equipment to a minimum—apart from a good, flat-bottomed wok and wok lid, all you need is an all-purpose chef's knife (or I like to use a Chinese cleaver), a chopping board, and a wooden spatula for stir-frying. Best to keep things simple, it's not about fancy equipment, but rather more robust, functional equipment that you will use time and time again.

COOK'S NOTES

Salt the oil

Some Chinese chefs swear that seasoning the oil with a pinch of salt before adding the aromatics helps to retain the color of the vegetables. It means the salt flavor is evenly distributed throughout, and you don't get any large, undissolved flakes of salt in the finished dish.

Meats

If you are on a budget, you can use less expensive cuts. These are usually tougher, but the trick is to use a couple of very small pinches of baking soda to tenderize the meat. My philosophy is to use free-range or organic where possible; yes, it is expensive, but I prefer quality over quantity. It is up to you whether you go for the cheaper or expensive meat option, just always make sure you season the meat first with a pinch of salt, ground white pepper, and a dusting of cornstarch to help the meat taste that much juicier. You can also add a pinch of Chinese five-spice, turmeric, dried chiles, fennel seeds, or ground coriander to inject flavor into the meat.

Water is your best friend

When the wok gets too hot to handle, water is your best friend. Having a small jug of water at hand, and knowing when to add a drop is important, especially if your ingredients are beginning to burn. If you are making a one-wok dish where you "don't return" (in Mandarin, *hui guo*) any ingredient to the wok, you will need to deglaze it after cooking individual ingredients, and you will need some liquid in between these additions to help each group of ingredients cook. Generally, this is after the protein, and again once the vegetables have gone in. When stir-frying tender leaf vegetables, after the oil and aromatics have gone in, adding a small amount of water around the edge of the wok will help to steam-cook the vegetables, ready for seasoning.

Quick homemade sauces & seasonings

From sriracha and oyster to garlic hoisin, you can create sweet, sour and spicy sauces that will complement your dishes, whether you use them as cook-in sauces or dressings on the side. Think of your condiment cupboard like a bar, where you are the mixologist, creating your own sauces.

Soybean pastes

I can't live without soybean pastes – the flavor combinations are limitless, with endless umami possibilities. My favorites include fermented salted dried black beans (soybeans dried and salted in the sun—just give them a rinse in water, then crush and mix into Shaohsing rice wine to make a paste), Japanese salty miso paste (which comes in red and white varieties—great for soups, stir-fries, sauces, dressings, and marinades), and the Korean chile paste *gochujang*.

Curry/Spice pastes

I love to experiment with South East Asian curry pastes such as Thai red curry, Thai green curry, yellow curry, and so on, and not just to make curry, but for stir-frying and in noodle soups. I also love chili pastes and sambals from Malaysia,

as well as spice mixes and tamarind paste, which give a sour kick and an exotic South East Asian taste to my dishes.

Cornstarch/Potato flour

This is an all-important pantry ingredient because it helps to bind the flavors in the wok to the protein and vegetables. Traditionally, a technique called "velveting" was the norm when cooking meat. It involved coating strips of meat with egg white and cornstarch to give it a silky texture when shallow-fried. However, I've designed a new way to enhance the flavor of the meat without

the shallow-frying step — I season the meat first with salt and ground white pepper, then dust with cornstarch or potato flour. This helps to seal in the juices as the meat hits the oil. The trick to making sure it doesn't stick to the wok is to let it brown for 10 seconds before flipping it to cook on the other side. Don't worry if the meat catches—those slightly burnt edges all add to the flavor. You can also loosen the flavors in the wok by using a small drop of water or Shaohsing rice wine to deglaze the pan.

In some of the dishes, the cornstarch is also mixed with cold water to create a blended paste that is usually added at the end of the cooking to thicken the sauce, and give it a shine. In others, where I group ingredients together for a more complex flavor, I like to add the cornstarch to the ingredients for the sauce—just ensure that the liquid, whether water or stock, is cold, so that the sauce doesn't thicken before it's added to the wok (you want the sauce to thicken and caramelize in the wok, not in the jug).

Dofu/Tofu

Dofu (which is the Mandarin name) or tofu (Japanese), is an excellent source of protein, iron, calcium, manganese, selenium and phosphorus, copper, magnesium, vitamin B1, and zinc. It also contains all nine essential amino acids. Available fresh, fried, firm and smoked, it's a great alternative for vegans and vegetarians—it features heavily in Buddhist Chinese cuisine. Try to get organic tofu, or that made from sprouted soy though—and stay away from GM soy.

Spices

To get the best out your spices, particularly whole ones like Sichuan peppercorns, first dry toast them in a wok or small pan, and then grind them in a mortar and pestle or clean coffee grinder.

Aromatics

Whether you do so with scallions, fresh cilantro, mint, raw bean sprouts, nuts, or seeds, Japanese nori seaweed, red pepper flakes, or a wedge of lemon or lime, adding a fragrant aromatic garnish to your stir-fry at the end will enhance your dish, so give it a go and experiment.

Rice & nutritious grains

For most of my dishes, unless it's a chow mein, jasmine rice is my rice of choice. You can also use other grains and pulses mixed into it, which is something I do when trying to eat more healthily. For example, I sometimes mix jasmine rice, wild rice and green lentils. Basmati is a good option for fried rice, as it is more robust. Brown rice is high in fiber, as well as being delicious, and can be mixed with jasmine rice, wild rice, and chickpeas to create a different bite.

Noodles

It's best to pre-cook noodles according to the package instructions, then drain and drizzle some toasted sesame oil over to prevent them from sticking together. For low-carb and wheat-free options, try mung bean noodles, soybean noodles, sweet potato noodles, *shirataki* and rice noodles. I also love the traditional wheat flour noodles, which come in several varieties, such as buckwheat, *somen*, *ramen*, *udon* and egg.

Eggs

All eggs used in these recipes are medium unless otherwise specified. Whenever possible, use organic or free-range chicken and eggs as they will taste so much better.

Gluten-free

Many dishes can be gluten-free if you omit wheat gluten/wheat flour noodles and use tamari instead of low-sodium light soy sauce. There are many gluten-free substitutes available at specialist producers online.

VEGAN &

VEGETARIAN

10 mins

11 mins

Ve GF DF

VIETNAMESE-STYLE GOLDEN TOFU NOODLE SALAD

3 x 2oz blocks dried mung bean thread noodles

1 tablespoon canola oil

2 cups peanut or sunflower oil

3½ oz fresh firm tofu, drained and sliced into ³/8-inch strips

scant ½ cup toasted cashew nuts

3oz blanched bean sprouts

mint leaves

1 small chile, seeded and finely chopped lengthwise

For the dressing

4 tablespoons *mirin* (rice wine)

2–3 tablespoons runny honey

2 tablespoons grated lemongrass

2 tablespoons tamari or low-sodium light soy sauce

4 mint leaves, shredded

4 tablespoons lime juice

2 small red chiles, seeded and chopped

This is a delicious and easy vegan noodle salad. If you are not vegan, you can use fish sauce instead of tamari; it will give a richness to the flavor. The slippery texture of mung bean noodles (also known as vermicelli glass noodles because of their translucent look) is great in this dish. Not only are they low in calories, they are also an absolute joy to eat! If you can't get hold of them, use vermicelli rice noodles, and if you don't eat honey, you can use golden syrup. Bon appetit!

Serves 4 kcal 390 carbs 55g protein 7.4g fat 15.9g

Cook the mung bean noodles in a pan of boiling water for 3 minutes, then drain and rinse under cold running water, and cut the noodles into 2-inch pieces. Place in a large bowl, cover with plastic wrap, and refrigerate. Drizzle over the canola oil to prevent the noodles from sticking together.

Combine all the dressing ingredients in a bowl, blend well, and set aside.

Heat a wok over high heat, fill to a third of its depth with peanut oil or sunflower oil. Heat the oil to 350°F, or until a bread cube dropped in the oil turns golden brown in 15 seconds and floats to the surface. Add the tofu strips, and fry for 8 minutes, until golden brown at the edges. Drain on a plate lined with paper towels.

Just before serving, toss the toasted cashew nuts, blanched bean sprouts, some of the mint leaves and the chopped chile into the noodles. Pour some of the dressing over the noodles, and toss all together. Transfer to bowls, then place the fried tofu on top, drizzle with more dressing, and garnish with more fresh mint. Serve immediately.

15 mins

6 mins

Oven time: 30–35 mins

Ve GF DF

THAI GREEN SWEET POTATO CURRY

10¹/₂oz sweet potatoes, cut into 1-inch chunks
pinch of salt
1–2 tablespoons canola oil

For the curry
1 tablespoon canola oil
1-inch piece of ginger, peeled and grated
2 small baby shallots, sliced, or ½ white onion, diced
1 stalk of lemongrass, any tough outer leaves discarded, cut into 1¹/₂-inch slices
2 tablespoons Thai green curry paste
1 tablespoon tamari or low-sodium light soy sauce
1 scant cup coconut milk
1¹/₄ cups vegetable stock
pinch of salt
3¹/₂oz snow peas, whole
Thai basil leaves
1 red chile, seeds in, sliced

This dish is great on a cold winter's day. First, roast the sweet potatoes, and then make a quick Thai green curry in the wok, and serve with jasmine rice. Perfect in every way, and so wholesome, yet easy to make, and above all—vegan too!

Serves 2 kcal 471 carbs 46.7g protein 5.1g fat 29.6g

Preheat the oven to 350°F. Put the sweet potatoes on a baking tray and season with the salt and oil. Roast in the oven for 30–35 minutes.

For the curry, heat a wok over medium heat, add the canola oil, and give the oil a swirl. Stir-fry the ginger, shallots or onion, and lemongrass for a few seconds to release their aroma.

Add the Thai green curry paste and tamari or light soy sauce, and stir around to distribute in the wok. Add the roast sweet potatoes, followed by the coconut milk and vegetable stock, and bring to a boil.

Add the salt and snow peas and cook for 30 seconds. Garnish with the basil and sliced chile. Spoon out and serve with Thai jasmine rice.

MOCK FISH CAKES WITH CRISP CHINESE VEGETABLES

1 tablespoon canola oil

2 garlic cloves, finely chopped

1-inch piece of ginger, peeled and grated

2oz carrots, cut into julienne strips

2oz baby corn, halved

2oz water chestnuts, drained

3oz broccoli, trimmed and cut into florets

3oz snow peas

3oz vegetarian fish cakes, halved

3oz bean sprouts, washed

3 scallions, sliced on an angle into 1-inch pieces

2 tablespoons toasted sesame oil

For the sauce

2 tablespoons tamari or low-sodium light soy sauce

2 tablespoons vegetarian oyster sauce

2 tablespoons cornstarch

2 tablespoons clear rice vinegar

1 scant cup cold vegetable stock

A simple and delicious stir-fry full of veggie goodness that, served with rice, makes a quick and healthy midweek supper.

Serves 2 kcal 372 carbs 40.4g protein 12.4g fat 21.2g

Combine all the ingredients for the sauce in a small cup, stir well, and set aside.

Heat a wok over high heat until the wok starts to smoke, then add the canola oil, and give the oil a swirl. Add the garlic and ginger, and stir-fry for 10 seconds. Add all the remaining vegetables from the carrots to the snow peas and stir-fry for an additional 2 minutes.

Stir the sauce mixture into the vegetables, then add the mock fish cakes, and stir-fry for another minute or so, until the liquid has thickened, and the vegetables are glazed but still crisp. Stir in the bean sprouts and scallions, and cook for another 20 seconds. Season with the sesame oil, and serve immediately with jasmine rice.

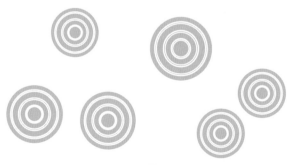

5 mins

9 mins

Ve DF

RED-COOKED TOFU WITH WHEAT FLOUR NOODLES

12oz fried tofu, whole, sliced into
½ inch chunks
pinch of salt
pinch of ground white pepper
1 tablespoon cornstarch or
potato flour
1 tablespoon peanut oil
1-inch piece of ginger, peeled and
sliced
1 tablespoon five-spice mix
(whole spices) including dried
tangerine peel and cinnamon
bark
1 tablespoon Shaohsing rice wine
or dry sherry
5oz dried wheat flour noodles,
cooked according to package
instructions, drained, drizzled
with toasted sesame oil
2 scallions, finely sliced, to
garnish

For the sauce
scant ½ cup cold vegetable
stock
3½ tablespoons tamari or low-
sodium light soy sauce
1 tablespoon dark soy sauce
1 tablespoon soft brown sugar
1 tablespoon cornstarch

This famous cooking technique is unique to eastern China and is used primarily for stews and braised dishes. My grandmother used to cook in this way with belly pork and also added boiled eggs.

It's not the dish itself that is red, but the liquid. It makes a simple and delicious supper. and is quick to cook, so I'm surprised it hasn't made its way onto takeout menus.

Serves 4 kcal 454 carbs 44g protein 26.2g fat 19.7g

Combine all the ingredients for the sauce in a bowl, mix well, and set aside.

Add the tofu to a bowl and season with the salt and white pepper, then add the cornstarch or potato flour and mix well.

Heat a wok over high heat until smoking, add the peanut oil and give the oil a swirl. Add the ginger and the five-spice mix, and stir-fry for a few seconds until fragrant, then add the tofu pieces and stir-fry for 2 minutes. Add the rice wine or dry sherry, and cook for another 2 minutes, then add the sauce.

Once the sauce has reduced and is slightly sticky, and a thicker consistency, take it off the heat.

Arrange the cooked noodles on serving plates, and top with the tofu mixture. Garnish with the scallions, and serve immediately.

20 mins

2 mins

V DF

SOY MUSHROOM CRISPY CHINESE EGGS

2 tablespoons canola oil

2 dried Chinese mushrooms, soaked in hot water for 15–20 minutes, drained, stalks discarded, sliced

1 teaspoon tamari or low-sodium light soy sauce

pinch of soft brown sugar

2 eggs

1 tablespoon chopped chives

To serve

1 tablespoon vegetarian oyster sauce mixed with 1 teaspoon sriracha chili sauce

This makes the perfect umami breakfast dish. I love meaty Chinese mushrooms—in fact, I always keep a glass jar of mushrooms soaking in the fridge for when I'm in need of a speedy dish such as this one. I think the dried Chinese mushrooms have so much earthier a flavor than fresh shiitake mushrooms, but it's up to you. Regardless, this is an easy and delicious mushroom egg-fry!

Serves 1 kcal 386 carbs 8.4g protein 15.4g fat 32.6g

Heat a wok over high heat, add 1 tablespoon of the canola oil, and give the oil a swirl. Add the Chinese mushroom slices, season with tamari or light soy sauce and soft brown sugar, and toss, cooking until brown and a little caramelized at the edges. Remove the mushrooms and transfer to a plate.

Wipe out the wok, reheat to medium-high heat, and add the remaining canola oil. Give the oil a swirl, then crack in the eggs. As the eggs cook for just under 1 minute, lay the mushrooms over the egg whites, then sprinkle with the chives, and cook until the bottom of each egg is crispy, and the egg yolks are runny. Transfer to a serving plate, and drizzle with the oyster and sriracha sauces mix.

10 mins

9 mins

Ve GF DF

SAUCY MUSHROOM AND GINGER TOFU

18oz fresh firm tofu, drained, and cut into 1-inch chunks

pinch of salt

pinch of ground white pepper

½ teaspoon Chinese five-spice powder

1 tablespoon tamari or low-sodium light soy sauce

1 tablespoon cornstarch or potato flour

1 tablespoon peanut oil

1-inch piece of ginger, peeled and sliced into matchsticks

5 large dried Chinese mushrooms, soaked in hot water for 20 minutes, drained, stalks discarded, cut into crescent slices

1 tablespoon Shaohsing rice wine or dry sherry

2 large scallions, sliced on the diagonal into 1-inch pieces

For the sauce

1 tablespoon tamari or low-sodium light soy sauce

1 tablespoon vegetarian oyster sauce

1 tablespoon chili sauce

scant ½ cup cold vegetable stock

1 tablespoon cornstarch or potato flour

This is one of my own flavor combinations—vegetarian oyster sauce with mushrooms! It's inspired by southern Chinese-style dishes from regions such as Canton and Fujian. So good, and vegan too. Sometimes, I add some baby bok choy in there for extra veg, it's up to you. Wok on! And yes, you guessed it—serve with jasmine rice!

Serves 2 kcal 378 carbs 31.2g protein 25.6g fat 17g

Place the tofu in a bowl and season with the salt, white pepper, five-spice powder, and tamari or light soy sauce. Dust with the cornstarch or potato flour and toss to mix.

Put all the sauce ingredients into another smaller bowl and stir to mix well.

Heat a wok over high heat, and when the wok starts to smoke, add the peanut oil. Add the ginger and mushrooms and stir-fry for a few seconds. Then add the tofu pieces, and stir-fry for 2–3 minutes, tossing gently for even cooking. Add the rice wine or dry sherry, and stir-fry for another 2 minutes, then add the sauce and bring to a boil. Stir-fry for 1 minute, then stir in the scallions. Remove from the heat and serve immediately.

5 mins

5 mins

Ve GF DF

WOK-FRIED ZUCCHINI WITH CORN AND CHILES

2 tablespoons canola oil

1-inch piece of ginger, peeled and grated

7oz baby zucchini, cut on the diagonal into ¼-inch slices

3 tablespoons Shaohsing rice wine or dry sherry

2 small jalapeño chiles, seeded and finely chopped

2 whole corn cobs, kernels sliced off

2 tablespoons tamari or low-sodium light soy sauce

1 tablespoon clear rice vinegar

dash of chili oil

1 tablespoon toasted sesame oil

1 large scallion, finely sliced, to garnish (optional)

This super delicious dish makes a quick and easy vegan midweek supper. The sauce the vegetables are wokked in, and the pops of pure sweetness from the corn, make this heavenly. Perfect with brown or jasmine rice.

Serves 2 kcal 280 carbs 16.2g protein 7.2g fat 21g

Heat a wok over high heat until smoking, add the canola oil, and give the oil a swirl. Add the ginger, and very quickly stir for a few seconds. Then add the zucchini, and toss for 1 minute. Add the rice wine or dry sherry, and if you're cooking on gas, try to catch the flame by tilting the wok (be careful when doing this).

Add the chiles and corn, and stir-fry for 1 minute. Then add the tamari or light soy sauce, vinegar, chili oil and sesame oil, and cook for another minute until all the corn kernels have softened, and turned a richer yellow. Give it a final stir, then transfer to a serving dish. Garnish with the scallion, if you like, and serve with brown or jasmine rice.

MOCK CHICKEN AND BROCCOLI "OYSTER" SAUCE CHOW MEIN

1 tablespoon canola oil

3 garlic cloves, minced

1-inch piece of ginger, peeled and grated

1 fresh red cayenne chile pepper, sliced (seeded, if you like)

7oz mock chicken, cut into strips

1 tablespoon Shaohsing rice wine or dry sherry

9oz broccolini, sliced on the diagonal into 1-inch pieces

1 tablespoon dark soy sauce

14oz cooked gluten- and egg-free noodles of your choice

large handful of bean sprouts

2 tablespoons tamari or low-sodium light soy sauce

1 tablespoon vegetarian oyster sauce or mushroom sauce

One of my favorite vegan suppers, this is ready in minutes. Use noodles of your choice in this one—I tend to go for thin wheat flour noodles or chunky udon noodles, depending on my mood. Children love this dish, and it's a great way to get them to eat broccoli.

Serves 2 kcal 576 carbs 89.4g protein 30.4g fat 11.6g

Heat a wok over high heat until smoking, add the canola oil, and give the oil a swirl. Quickly add the garlic, ginger, and chile, and stir-fry for a few seconds. Add the mock chicken, and stir-fry together for a few seconds.

As the mock chicken starts to brown at the edges, add the rice wine or dry sherry, and follow quickly with the broccolini. Stir-fry for 30 seconds, then add the dark soy sauce and toss well.

Add the cooked noodles, and give it a good mix, then add the bean sprouts. Toss together, then season with the tamari or light soy sauce and vegetarian oyster sauce and cook, tossing and stirring, for less than 1 minute. Serve immediately.

5 mins

9 mins

Ve DF

SICHUAN CHILE TOMATO MOCK CHICKEN

1 tablespoon peanut oil

2 garlic cloves, crushed

1 tablespoon roughly sliced, peeled ginger

1 red chile, seeded and finely chopped

1 tablespoon Sichuan peppercorns

1 tablespoon chili bean paste

12oz mock chicken, cut into 3/8-inch strips

1 tablespoon Shaohsing rice wine or dry sherry

2 large, ripe heirloom tomatoes, skin on and each quartered (see tip)

2 scallions, sliced on the diagonal into 1-inch lengths

For the sauce

1 tablespoon tamari or low-sodium light soy sauce

2/3 cup cold vegetable stock

2 tablespoons cornstarch

I really like Sichuan peppercorns—their mouthwatering, numbing spice is addictive. Ripe heirloom tomatoes are another favorite, so this is a pairing of two of my favorite ingredients.

Serves 2 kcal 350 carbs 36.2g protein 21g fat 11.6g

Combine all the ingredients for the sauce in a bowl and mix well.

Heat a wok over high heat, and as the wok starts to smoke, add the peanut oil and give it a swirl. Add the garlic, ginger, chile, Sichuan peppercorns, and chili bean paste, and stir well for less than 1 minute. Add the mock chicken, and cook for 10 seconds, then add the rice wine or dry sherry, and cook for about 1 minute, stirring continuously. Add the heirloom tomatoes, and stir together.

Add the sauce and bring to a boil, then add the scallions and cook for 15 seconds. Transfer to serving plates, and serve immediately with jasmine rice.

Ching's Tip

No need to peel the tomatoes. The skin holds all the nutrients.

10 mins

5 mins

Ve DF

SICHUAN MOCK CHICKEN AND ZUCCHINI STIR-FRY

1 tablespoon canola oil

2 small garlic cloves, roughly chopped

1-inch piece of ginger, peeled, and finely grated

1 large red cayenne chile pepper, seeded and sliced

7oz baby zucchini, cut on the diagonal into 2-inch slices

2 pieces of mock chicken, sliced thinly on the diagonal into 2-inch slices

For the Sichuan spicy sauce

1 tablespoon chili bean paste

2 tablespoons Chinkiang black rice vinegar or balsamic vinegar

1 tablespoon tamari or low-sodium light soy sauce

1 teaspoon soft brown sugar

1 tablespoon cornstarch

1 tablespoon Shaohsing rice wine or dry sherry

1 teaspoon toasted sesame oil

My go-to recipe time and time again, this is a quick and easy vegan stir-fry that is ready in a matter of minutes. Mock chicken—fried wheat gluten—can be bought from Chinese supermarkets or you can use a chunky vegan soy protein of your choice. Serve with jasmine rice.

Serves 2 kcal 306 carbs 27g protein 18g fat 11.8g

Combine all the ingredients for the sauce in a bowl and mix well.

Heat a wok over high heat until smoking, add the canola oil, and give the oil a swirl. Add the garlic, ginger, chile, and zucchini, and toss for 1 minute, then add a small splash of cold water around the edge of the wok to help create some steam. Add the mock chicken, and toss together for 30 seconds until the mock chicken is warmed through.

Pour in the sauce, bring to a boil and coat the ingredients well. Then give the dish a final stir, take it off the heat, and serve immediately with steamed rice.

10 mins

6 mins

Ve GF DF

FRIED TOFU AND BABY BOK CHOY IN VEGETARIAN OYSTER SAUCE

2 tablespoons peanut oil
2 garlic cloves, roughly chopped
1-inch piece of ginger, peeled and grated
1 red cayenne chile pepper (seed one half and leave seeds in the other half), sliced
7oz firm tofu pieces, sliced into 1-inch chunks
12oz bok choy, leaves separated
small handful of shimeji mushrooms, trimmed
2 tablespoons vegetarian oyster sauce or mushroom sauce
1 tablespoon Shaohsing rice wine or dry sherry
1 teaspoon dark soy sauce
1 tablespoon tamari or low-sodium light soy sauce
1 tablespoon clear rice vinegar
1 tablespoon toasted sesame oil
1 large scallion, greens sliced, to garnish

This is a variation of my favorite saucy stir-fry, although this is more of a dry-fry. It makes a healthy dinner in minutes, and is perfect with an array of other dishes to share, or to have on its own with noodles or rice.

Serves 2 kcal 310 carbs 14.2g protein 13.8g fat 21.4g

Heat a wok over high heat until smoking, add the peanut oil, and give the oil a swirl. Add the garlic, ginger, and chile, and stir-fry for a few seconds, then add the tofu. Cook, stirring, for less than 1 minute, then add the bok choy leaves. Toss for a few seconds, then add the mushrooms and a few splashes of cold water around the edge of the wok to create some steam to help the vegetables cook.

Make a well in the center of the vegetables, and season with the vegetarian oyster sauce, the rice wine or dry sherry, the dark soy sauce, tamari or light soy sauce, and vinegar, then toss the vegetables to coat them well.

Lastly, season with the sesame oil, and remove from the heat. Transfer to a serving dish, garnish with the scallion, and serve with steamed jasmine rice.

5 mins

2–3 mins

Ve DF

SPICED MOCK CHICKEN WITH SNOW PEAS

1 tablespoon canola oil

1-inch piece of ginger, peeled and grated

10½oz snow peas

7oz mock chicken, cut into strips

1 teaspoon chili bean paste

1 teaspoon tamari or low-sodium light soy sauce

pinch of soft brown sugar

4 tablespoons roasted salted cashews

A simple stir-fry of snow peas with cashew nuts, this can be served as a side dish or as a meal for two. If you are watching your salt intake, use raw cashew nuts rather than salted. Chili bean paste is available from good Chinese grocers and online, but if you can't get it leave it out.

Serves 2 kcal 337 carbs 16.9g protein 17.7g fat 18.8g

Heat a wok over high heat until smoking, add the canola oil, and give it a swirl. Add the ginger, and allow to sizzle for 30 seconds, then add the snow peas and stir-fry for 1–2 minutes. Add the mock chicken, and season with the chili bean paste, tamari or light soy sauce and brown sugar. Toss well, then sprinkle in the cashews and serve immediately.

SICHUAN SPICY SALT AND PEPPER MOCK DUCK

10½oz jasmine rice, rinsed until water runs clear

12oz mock duck, cut into ⅜-inch strips

few pinches of ground white pepper

1 tablespoon cornstarch or potato flour

2 tablespoons canola oil

1 tablespoon mirin

1 teaspoon Sichuan peppercorns, crushed

bunch of scallions, cut into 2-inch pieces (optional)

2 tablespoons tamari or low-sodium light soy sauce

few pinches of cracked black pepper

2 teaspoons chili oil

juice of 1 lime

2 teaspoons toasted sesame seeds

1 red chile, deseeded and finely chopped, to garnish

This is a stir-fry dish inspired by Sichuan in China. The hot chili oil and spices warm the senses, and make an elegant, quick, and inexpensive dish for entertaining when served with plain rice. Scallions are the choice of veg here, but if you don't like them, substitute with a veg of your choice.

Serves 4 kcal 454 carbs 74.4g protein 18.1g fat 11.2g

Place the rice in a medium pan, add 17fl oz water, and bring to a boil. Turn the heat to low, put the lid on, and keep on a gentle simmer for 20 minutes until the grains are cooked, then fluff with a fork.

Meanwhile, season the mock duck with a few pinches of salt, the pepper, and cornstarch or potato flour.

Heat a wok over high heat until smoking, add the canola oil, and give the oil a swirl. Add the mock duck pieces, and stir-fry for 1 minute. Deglaze the wok with the mirin. Add the Sichuan peppercorns and scallions, if using, and toss them all together, stirring for 20 seconds. Add the tamari or light soy sauce, and season with a few pinches of salt and black pepper. Stir in the chili oil, lime juice, and toasted sesame seeds. Transfer to serving plates, garnish with the chile and serve immediately with the rice.

10 mins

5 mins

V GF DF

EGGY TOMATO CABBAGE HO FUN

3 eggs

1 tablespoon cornstarch, blended with 2 tablespoons cold water

1 tablespoon canola oil

2 garlic cloves, grated

2 red chiles, seeded and finely chopped

¼ white cabbage, finely shredded

3 large ripe tomatoes, quartered

3 ½oz canned chopped tomatoes

1 tablespoon Shaohsing rice wine or dry sherry

3 generous tablespoons vegetable stock

5 ½oz brown wide rice noodles, soaked in warm water for 10 minutes, drained

2 tablespoons tamari or low-sodium light soy sauce

2 scallions, finely sliced on the diagonal, to garnish

This is an eggy, tomatoey, delicious veggie stir-fry, perfect for adults and kids alike. It's pure comfort food, and great for a snack or dinner. For an extra kick, serve with some sriracha chili sauce. For vegans, lose the eggs, and instead add meaty shiitake mushrooms and more scallions.

Serves 2 kcal 563 carbs 90.7g protein 22.6g fat 14.2g

Beat the eggs in a small bowl, then stir in the blended cornstarch.

Heat a wok over high heat until smoking, add the canola oil, and give it a swirl. Add the garlic and chiles, and stir-fry for a few seconds to release their aroma. Add the cabbage and stir-fry for 30 seconds. Add the fresh tomatoes, and wok-fry for 10 seconds, then add the canned tomatoes, and season the mixture with the rice wine or dry sherry. Add the vegetable stock, and as the sauce starts to reduce, quickly add the noodles and toss for 30 seconds.

Make a well in the center of the mixture, pour in the beaten egg mixture, and mix together to scramble. Toss all the ingredients together, season with the tamari or light soy sauce, garnish with the scallions, and serve immediately.

5 mins

5 mins

Ve GF DF

SOY BEAN SPROUT CILANTRO CHEUNG FUN ROLLS

2 tablespoons canola oil

14oz fresh *cheung fun rice* noodle rolls (cigar-shaped about 3/8-inch thick) or pre-soaked brown rice wide noodles

2 tablespoons tamari or low-sodium light soy sauce

2 tablespoons vegetarian oyster sauce

7oz bean sprouts

1 teaspoon toasted sesame oil

pinch of ground white pepper

large handful of cilantro, roughly chopped

Nothing screams Asian comfort food more than delicious fat *cheung fun* rice noodle rolls—delicious, silky, and perfect when steamed and dressed with a sweet soy sauce. However, I like mine wok-fried in a good-quality soy sauce, with some crunchy bean sprouts and fresh cilantro. Simple and addictive. If you can't get *cheung fun* rolls (usually found in the fresh section of Chinese supermarkets) go for dried, flat, wide rice noodles like pad Thai noodles. It won't be the same experience, but it will still be delicious. This is a favorite with my vegan friends too.

Serves 2 kcal 526 carbs 83.8g protein 9.8g fat 18.2g

Heat a wok over high heat until smoking, add the canola oil, and give the oil a swirl. Add the noodle rolls, and wok-fry for 20 seconds, then season with the tamari or light soy sauce. Add the vegetarian oyster sauce and bean sprouts, and toss for a few seconds to mix well. Season with the sesame oil and white pepper, then stir in the chopped cilantro, and eat immediately.

5 mins

3 mins

Ve GF DF

WOK-FRIED GINGER SOY BOK CHOY WITH CRISPY SHALLOTS

1 tablespoon canola oil

pinch of sea salt flakes

1 teaspoon peeled and grated ginger

7oz baby bok choy (5–6 small heads), each head quartered

1 tablespoon Shaohsing rice wine or dry sherry

1 teaspoon Chinkiang black rice vinegar or balsamic vinegar

1 teaspoon tamari or low-sodium light soy sauce

½ teaspoon cornstarch, blended with 1 teaspoon cold water

½ teaspoon toasted sesame oil

small handful of deep-fried sliced shallots, to garnish (optional)

One of my all-time favorite go-to vegetable dishes. Bok choy, which translates as "white vegetable", belongs to the same family as the cabbage, and has two types—white-stemmed and green-stemmed. Both are equally delicious when wokked up in this way.

Serves 2 kcal 146 carbs 9.1g protein 2.3g fat 11g

Heat a wok over high heat until smoking, add the canola oil, and give it a swirl. Season the oil with the salt, then add the ginger, and stir-fry for a couple of seconds. Add the bok choy, and toss for less than 1 minute. Season with the rice wine or dry sherry, the vinegar, and tamari or light soy sauce, then drizzle in the blended cornstarch. Add the sesame oil, and give it one last toss. Pour out onto serving plates, garnish with some crushed fried shallots, if you like, and serve immediately.

10 mins

5 mins

Ve GF DF

ADDICTIVE CRISPY SEAWEED

sunflower oil, for deep-frying
7oz bok choy, stems removed and finely shredded
pinches of sea salt, to taste
pinches of granulated sugar, to taste
1 tablespoon toasted sesame seeds, to garnish

This is not served in China, but is a Western Chinese dish invented by Chinese cooks. It doesn't actually contain seaweed, but is made with finely shredded bok choy leaves that are deep-fried. I like to season mine with salt and granulated sugar, so that it's both sweet and salty.

It's a great way to use up any leftover bok choy you have that may have wilted. If you're neither vegan nor vegetarian, this is also great as an appetizer, or sprinkled as a garnish over crispy squid.

Serves 4 kcal 48 carbs 1.2g protein 1.2g fat 4.1g

Heat a wok over high heat. Fill the wok to a third of its depth with the oil and heat to 350°F. Add half the bok choy leaves and deep-fry for a few seconds, then lift out using a spider, and drain on paper towels. Cook the rest of the bok choy in the same way. Season the seaweed with salt and sugar, transfer to a serving dish, and sprinkle on some toasted sesame seeds. Serve immediately.

JAPANESE RICE OMELET (OMU-RAISU)

For the rice filling
1 tablespoon canola oil

1 small white onion, diced

2oz smoked tofu, sliced, or smoked thick-cut bacon, diced

½ red bell pepper, seeded and diced

½ green bell pepper, seeded and diced

4 white mushrooms, diced

12oz (about 3 cups) cooked jasmine rice

3 tablespoons tomato ketchup

1 tablespoon tamari or low-sodium light soy sauce

pinch of sea salt

pinch of ground white pepper

For the omelets (makes 2)
2 tablespoons canola oil

6 eggs

2 pinches each of sea salt and ground white pepper

To serve
sriracha chili sauce

mixed salad leaves or romaine lettuce leaves

Rice is truly versatile—it can be stir-fried, cooked as a soup, steamed, and made into rice parcel dumplings; and, of course, it's an accompaniment for curries, too. In this quick and easy-to-make Japanese snack, rice accompanies eggs to make a delicious rice omelet.

Serves 2 kcal 692 carbs 63.1g protein 33.2g fat 36g

Heat a wok over high heat until smoking, add the canola oil, and give the oil a swirl. Add the onion, and wok-fry for 15 seconds until golden and translucent, then add the smoked tofu or thick-cut diced bacon, and stir-fry for 30 seconds. Add the red and green bell peppers, and the mushrooms, and stir-fry for another minute. Tip in the cooked rice, and stir-fry for an additional minute.

Season with the ketchup, tamari or light soy sauce, salt and white pepper. Transfer to an ovenproof dish. Keep covered in the oven on low heat.

To make the omelets, wipe out the wok, then reheat over medium heat, add half the canola oil, and give the oil a swirl. Beat 3 of the eggs, add a pinch of salt and white pepper, and spread the egg mixture in an even layer in the wok. When the omelet is almost cooked, place half the fried rice on one half and fold the omelet over the rice. Keep covered and warm in the low oven while you repeat with the remaining oil, eggs, and rice.

Serve the omelets with a side of sriracha chili sauce, and some mixed salad leaves.

8 mins

6 mins

Ve GF DF

VEGGIE "PORK" MINCE WITH FRENCH BEANS

1 tablespoon canola oil

2 garlic cloves, minced

1 red chile, seeded and finely chopped

10oz rehydrated textured vegetable protein (TVP)

½ teaspoon Chinese five-spice powder

1 teaspoon dark soy sauce

1 tablespoon Shaohsing rice wine or dry sherry

5oz French beans (thin green beans) or wax beans, sliced on the diagonal into 1¼-inch pieces

3½ tablespoons cold vegetable stock

1 tablespoon tamari or low-sodium light soy sauce

1 tablespoon Chinkiang black rice vinegar or balsamic vinegar

1 teaspoon cornstarch, blended with 1 tablespoon cold water

pinch of ground white pepper

1 teaspoon toasted sesame oil

½ teaspoon chili oil

handful of cilantro, to garnish

This is such a satisfying vegan supper. Textured vegetable protein is made from soybeans, and makes a delicious meaty substitute. Some come dried, and others already rehydrated (like Quorn). I use the Clearspring brand, which is dried, so you need to follow the package instructions to rehydrate it. French beans are super sweet and crunchy—a great veg for all year round. Perfect on rice or noodles.

Serves 2 kcal 514 carbs 25.5g protein 67.4g fat 16.5g

Heat a wok over high heat until smoking, add the canola oil, and give the oil a swirl. Add the garlic and chile, and toss for a few seconds to release their flavors. Add the textured vegetable protein, and let it settle in the wok for 30 seconds to brown and sear, then stir-fry for 1 minute. Add the five-spice powder, and season with the dark soy sauce. Toss until the ground TVP turns a rich brown color, then season and deglaze the wok with the rice wine or dry sherry. Add the French beans, and toss for 2 minutes.

Add the vegetable stock, and bring to a boil, then season with the tamari or light soy sauce and vinegar. Stir in the blended cornstarch to give the dish a shine, then add a pinch of white pepper. Season with the toasted sesame oil and chili oil, and garnish with the cilantro before serving.

5 mins

1 hr
5 mins

Ve GF DF

CLASSIC PLAIN CONGEE "ZHOU"

9oz (scant 1½ cups) uncooked
   jasmine rice
¼ cup glutinous rice (optional)
1 cup vegetable stock
salt (optional)

Although in my family congee is eaten mainly for breakfast or lunch, it can also be eaten at dinner time. Congee mainly consists of two types of rice—short-grain, and some glutinous rice for a stickier, thicker consistency. If you have some glutinous rice in your pantry, then by all means add ¼ cup of it to the recipe, otherwise leave it out. This is, of course, a more classic congee, where it is very slowly cooked on the stove. For a cheat and speedy congee, see page 187. To make it vegan, just substitute the beef with tofu strips or mock duck pieces instead.

If you like, you can add cooked mung beans and split yellow peas in with the cooked congee at the end. Whenever I had an upset stomach, my grandmother would give me a steaming bowl of salted congee and I would feel like I would live to see another day!

Serves 4 kcal 237 carbs 56.4g protein 5.3g fat 0.6g

Place the rice in a strainer and wash under running water until the water runs clear. Drain well, and pour into a large wok.

Add a generous 3 cups water and the vegetable stock, and bring to a boil over high heat. Once boiling, turn the heat to medium, put a lid on top of the wok, and cook for 1 hour, stirring occasionally to make sure the rice does not stick to the side and bottom of the wok. Cook until it forms a thick rice porridge. If you prefer yours with a thinner consistency, add more hot water. Serve as an accompaniment.

Ching's Tip
Add salt if you have a stomach ache – trust me: it's an age-old remedy and it works!

MOCK PORK CONGEE

8 mins

+ 20 minutes soaking for dried Chinese mushrooms

3 mins

Ve DF

1 tablespoon canola oil

2 shallots, finely diced

4 dried Chinese mushrooms, soaked in hot water for 20 minutes, drained and diced

5 chunky pieces of vegetarian mock pork, diced

2 celery stalks, finely diced

2 tablespoons tamari or low-sodium light soy sauce

1 recipe quantity cooked Classic Plain Congee "Zhou" (page 52)

pinch of sea salt

pinch of ground white pepper

1 tablespoon toasted sesame oil

2 dried nori sheets, shredded

1 scallion, finely chopped

I love Chinese "ham" or "*shu-rou*" (plant/tree meat) as we call it in Mandarin. If you can't get it, vegetarian mock pork is equally good and delicious.

The mix of textures here is great—the chewiness of the earthy Chinese mushrooms, the crunchy texture of the celery, and the bite of the seaweed.

Serves 2 kcal 420 carbs 48g protein 22.3g fat 16.8g

Heat a wok over high heat until smoking, add the canola oil, and give it a swirl. Add the shallots, and stir-fry for 1 minute until translucent. Add the Chinese mushrooms, mock pork, and celery, and stir-fry for 2 minutes until aromatic, then season with the soy sauce.

Add this to the cooked congee, and stir in well. Season with the salt, white pepper, and toasted sesame oil. Stir in the shredded nori, add the scallion, and serve immediately.

15 mins

5–6 mins

Ve DF

SPICED VEGAN LARB LETTUCE CUPS

1 tablespoon canola oil
7oz textured vegetable protein (TVP)
1 fresh kaffir lime leaf, very finely sliced into strips, or use freshly grated lime zest
1 tablespoon tamari or low-sodium light soy sauce
pinch of ground white pepper
pinch of dried red pepper flakes
juice of ½ lime

For the spice mixture
1 teaspoon ground Sichuan peppercorns
1 teaspoon ground cumin
¼ teaspoon cloves
1 teaspoon vegetable bouillon powder
¼ teaspoon star anise
1 teaspoon ground jasmine rice
¼ teaspoon dried red pepper flakes

To assemble
1 small cucumber, cut on a deep angle into 1¼-inch slices
hoisin sauce, for dipping
2–3 Little Gem lettuces, leaves separated from the stalk
1 small carrot, cut into julienne strips
1 tablespoon fresh chive pieces
1 lime, quartered

This Chinese-Laos dish is a spiced vegetable stir-fry using textured vegetable protein (TVP) as the meat substitute and some aromatic seasonings, then served in fresh, crunchy, Little Gem lettuce cups. It is my vegan version of "spiced larb" (a meat salad generally considered the unofficial national dish of Laos). Make a large batch of the spice mix, and then store the rest in a small glass jar to use on another occasion. It may seem like a long list of ingredients, but I promise you'll find most in your pantry. This makes a delicious appetizer, or you can turn it into a main dish—I often like to tear the lettuce into pieces, then pour the hot spiced stir-fry over it, and eat it like a hot/cold salad. Delicious!

Serves 4 kcal 189 carbs 10.5g protein 24.4g fat 6.7g

Toast all the ingredients for the spice mixture in a dry wok until fragrant, then place in a mortar and pestle (or use a clean coffee grinder) and grind to a powder.

Heat a wok over high heat until smoking, add the canola oil, and give it a swirl. Add 1 teaspoon of the spice mixture and toast for a few seconds, then add the textured vegetable protein, and wok-fry together until dry, crisp, and golden. Add the kaffir lime strips or lime zest, and season with the tamari or light soy sauce, the white pepper, red pepper flakes, and lime juice.

To assemble a lettuce cup, dip a few cucumber slices in some hoisin sauce, place in a lettuce leaf, top with a couple of carrot strips, spiced vegan "larb", and chives, and eat immediately, served with the lime wedges on the side. You can either assemble the individual cups, or I like to serve all the elements separately, and let everyone build their own.

VEGAN PHO

1-inch piece of ginger, peeled and
    left whole
2 stalks of lemongrass, sliced
3 red onions, halved
2 small carrots, sliced on the
    diagonal into 3/8-inch slices
8 cherry tomatoes
3 1/2oz Napa cabbage, sliced
2 tablespoons vegetable bouillon
    powder
1 star anise
3 1/2oz mixed fresh mushrooms—
    shiitake, enoki, oyster
3 1/2oz fresh corn cob, sliced in
    1-inch rounds
2 x 3 1/2oz blocks dried instant
    vermicelli rice noodles or flat
    rice noodles
1 teaspoon sriracha chili sauce
large pinch of sea salt
large pinch of ground white
    pepper
juice of 2 limes
3 1/2oz fried tofu slices or smoked
    tofu slices
3 1/2oz bean sprouts
1 scallion, sliced

For the garnish and to serve
handful each of fresh Thai basil,
    mint, and cilantro leaves
1 red chile, sliced
sriracha chili sauce

This is clean, refreshing, and restorative, and uses a basic
"cheat" pho broth. You can add as much spice to it as you like,
and vary the vegetables. I could eat it any time of the year.

If using flat rice noodles, soak them in warm water for
5 minutes, then drain.

Serves 2 kcal 428 carbs 71.7g protein 18.5g fat 8.2g

Heat a wok over medium heat, add the ginger, lemongrass, red
onions, and carrots, and char-brown for 1–2 minutes. Then add
5 1/4 cups water, the tomatoes, Napa cabbage, bouillon powder,
and star anise, and simmer for 5 minutes until the cabbage
leaves have wilted, and the tomatoes have softened and are
ready to burst.

Add the mushrooms, corn, and noodles, and simmer for
1–2 minutes.

Season with the chili sauce, salt, white pepper, and lime juice,
and stir in well. Stir in the tofu slices and bean sprouts, and
sprinkle the scallion over.

Divide between two bowls, and garnish with the basil, mint,
and cilantro leaves and the chile slices. Serve with sriracha on
the side.

VEGAN SQUASH, TURNIP AND CARROT BROTH WITH CILANTRO

2 tablespoons vegetable bouillon powder

9oz winter squash flesh, cut into 1-inch pieces, blanched and drained

1-inch piece of ginger, peeled and sliced into matchsticks

7oz daikon, (Asian radish), sliced into ⅜-inch rounds each, then cut into 6 wedges

2 carrots, cut into ⅜-inch rounds, and then quartered into wedges

1 tablespoon Shaohsing rice wine or dry sherry

pinch of sea salt

pinch of ground white pepper

handful of roughly chopped cilantro leaves

This is one of my grandfather's favorite recipes. The light, sweet broth is not overpowering, and the daikon adds a slight bittersweetness. The cilantro adds an aromatic fragrance at the end. It reminds me of my grandmother's home-style cooking. I hope you like this as much as I do. It's perfect for a light supper, and is super healthy too.

Serves 4 kcal 62 carbs 11.8g protein 2.2g fat 0.9g

Bring a generous 1½ quarts water to a boil in a wok, then stir in the bouillon powder until dissolved. Add the squash, ginger, daikon, carrots, and rice wine or dry sherry, and simmer over low heat for 20 minutes, until the squash, daikon and carrots are tender. Season with salt and white pepper. Just before serving, add the chopped cilantro and serve immediately. Perfect spooned over cooked jasmine rice for a delicious rice soup.

20 mins

10 mins

Ve GF DF

VEGAN GOLDEN SPICED TURMERIC TOFU WITH ASPARAGUS, SHIITAKE AND CHICKPEA FRIED RICE

For the fried rice
10½oz brown rice
1¼ cups vegetable stock
7oz canned chickpeas, drained and rinsed

For the turmeric tofu
14oz block of fresh firm tofu, drained, cut into ⅝-inch squares
pinch of sea salt
pinch of ground white pepper
pinch each of ground turmeric, red pepper flakes, ground cumin, ground fennel
1 tablespoon cornstarch
2 tablespoons canola oil

For the vegetables
1 tablespoon canola oil
1 garlic clove, minced
1 teaspoon peeled and finely grated ginger
1 red chile, seeded and finely chopped
1 small carrot, finely diced
2oz asparagus spears, diced
6 fresh shiitake mushrooms, stems discarded, sliced
2 tablespoons tamari or low-sodium light soy sauce
2 tablespoons vegetarian oyster sauce
1 teaspoon toasted sesame oil

For the garnish
1 scallion, finely chopped
small handful of cilantro leaves, chopped

If you are vegan, this rice dish will hopefully send you to heaven!

Serves 4 kcal 511 carbs 75.6g protein 19.8g fat 16.2g

Wash the rice until the water runs clear, place with the stock and 1½ cups water in a medium pan, bring to a boil, then turn the heat down to low, cover with a lid, and cook for 15 minutes. Pour in the chickpeas and stir, then cover and keep warm until ready to stir-fry.

Place the tofu pieces in a shallow bowl, sprinkle with the salt, white pepper, turmeric, red pepper flakes, cumin, fennel, and cornstarch, and turn gently to coat.

Heat a wok over medium heat, add the canola oil, and give the oil a swirl. Add the tofu, and wok-fry on each side for 2 minutes until seared and golden, using a flat knife or spatula to help you turn the tofu gently without breaking up the pieces. Transfer to a warm plate, cover and keep in an oven set to low heat until ready to serve.

Clean the wok and reheat over high heat until smoking. Add the canola oil, and swirl the oil around, then add the garlic, ginger, and chile, and stir for a few seconds until fragrant. Add the diced carrot, and stir for 2 minutes or until tender. Toss in the asparagus and shiitake mushrooms, and stir-fry for another minute. Season with the tamari or light soy sauce, vegetarian oyster sauce, and the sesame oil and stir well. Toss the chickpea rice in, and mix well. Adjust the seasoning, adding more soy or vegetarian oyster sauce to taste. Top with the turmeric tofu, garnish with the scallion and cilantro, and serve.

3 mins

8 mins

V DF

CANTONESE-STYLE EGG AND TOMATO MACARONI NOODLE SOUP

3 ripe tomatoes, sliced

1 tablespoon vegetable bouillon powder

7oz canned plum tomatoes, retain juices from the can

3 eggs, lightly beaten

1 tablespoon tamari or low-sodium light soy sauce

dash of toasted sesame oil

pinch of sea salt

pinch of ground white pepper

1 tablespoon sriracha chili sauce (to taste)

10 ½oz cooked macaroni, drained, dressed in a little canola oil

1 tablespoon cornstarch blended with 2 tablespoons cold water

large handful of baby spinach (optional)

2 scallions, finely sliced

A classic comfort dish served in many of the licensed street vendors (*dai pai dongs*) offering Hong Kongers a quick snack. Add a good amount of sriracha for a kicked-up version. This is pure comfort in a bowl, and yes, you read correctly, you'll want canned plum tomatoes for a rich, tart flavor.

Serves 2 kcal 473 carbs 75.3g protein 22.8g fat 11g

If you want to skin the fresh tomatoes before chopping, cut a small cross at the base of each one. Plunge them into a wok or pan of boiling water for less than 1 minute, then drain. The skin will peel off easily. Finely chop the flesh, discarding the hard center. However, most of the nutrients are underneath the skin, so I don't bother—also it does make the dish even quicker to prepare.

Pour 3½ cups boiling water into a wok, and bring back to a boil. Stir in the bouillon powder, and bring to a simmer, then add the fresh tomatoes, and cook over medium heat for 5 minutes until the tomatoes have softened. Add the canned plum tomatoes with their juice, and bring to a simmer. Pour the beaten eggs into the broth, stirring gently. Add the tamari or light soy sauce, sesame oil, salt, white pepper, sriracha chili sauce, cooked macaroni and blended cornstarch, and mix well. If using, add the baby spinach and let it wilt, then garnish with the scallions, and serve immediately.

+ 20 mins to soak
wood ear mushrooms

15 mins

Ve GF DF

VEGAN TRADITIONAL HOT AND SOUR SOUP

1 tablespoon vegetable bouillon powder

1 tablespoon peeled and grated ginger

2 chiles, seeded and finely chopped

1 teaspoon Shaohsing rice wine or dry sherry

1 tablespoon dark soy sauce

7oz Napa cabbage, shredded

1 x 8oz can bamboo shoots, drained and cut into strips

¾ cup dried wood ear mushrooms, soaked in hot water for 20 minutes, drained and finely sliced

3½oz fresh firm tofu, drained, cut into 2-inch x ⅜-inch strips

2oz Sichuan preserved vegetables in chili oil, rinsed and sliced (optional)

2 tablespoons tamari or low-sodium light soy sauce

3 tablespoons Chinkiang black rice or balsamic vinegar

1 tablespoon chili oil

2 pinches of ground white pepper

1 tablespoon cornstarch, blended with 2 tablespoons cold water

3½oz enoki mushrooms, ends discarded, cut into 1-inch slices

1 large scallion, finely sliced

chopped cilantro, to serve

The spicy chiles, the sourness of the earthy black rice vinegar, the softness of the tofu, and the crunchy wood ear mushrooms and bamboo shoots make this one of my all-time favorite soup recipes—and the best thing is that it's my husband's favorite too, so whenever I get into trouble with him, all is forgiven if I make this. It may look like a long list of ingredients, but trust me, it's a one-wok situation and everything goes in. To make it into a more substantial meal just add noodles or pour over steamed rice.

Serves 4 kcal 128 carbs 15.6g protein 5.8g fat 4.8g

Pour 1 quart water into a wok and bring to a boil. Add the bouillon powder, and stir to dissolve. Bring back to a boil, then add all the ingredients up to the tofu, including the wood ear mushrooms. Boil for 3 minutes, then turn the heat down to medium, and add the tofu, preserved vegetables (or leave out if you don't have any), tamari or light soy sauce. vinegar, chili oil and white pepper and simmer for 10 minutes.

Stir in the blended cornstarch to thicken the soup (add more if you like a thicker consistency). Drop in the enoki mushrooms, scallion, and cilantro, and serve immediately.

20 mins

+ 1 hour marinating

10 mins

Ve DF

VEGAN CRISPY "BOTTOM" "GUO TIEH" VEGETABLE DUMPLINGS

3½oz carrots, finely diced

3½oz dried shiitake mushrooms, soaked in hot water for 20 minutes, drained and finely chopped

6oz smoked tofu

1 teaspoon salt

¼ teaspoon ground white pepper

½ teaspoon superfine sugar

¼ teaspoon toasted sesame oil

¼ teaspoon tamari or low-sodium light soy sauce

½ vegetable stock cube, grated

¼ teaspoon Shaohsing rice wine or dry sherry

1-inch piece of ginger, peeled and grated

4oz Napa cabbage, finely shredded

2–3 scallions, finely diced

3oz canned water chestnuts, drained, and finely diced

1 tablespoon cornstarch

1 package (30) wheat flour gyoza dumpling wrappers

1 tablespoon canola oil

1 tablespoon all-purpose flour

60 chives, to garnish

*per dumpling

These Cantonese-style pot-stickers are perfect party food. You can leave them in the pan and keep covered warm until ready to serve, or you can serve them straight from the pan.

Makes 30 kcal 48 carbs 8.1g protein 2g fat 1.1g*

Mix the carrots, mushrooms, and tofu with the salt, white pepper, sugar, sesame oil, soy sauce, grated stock cube, rice wine or dry sherry, and grated ginger. Add the cabbage, scallions, and water chestnuts, and use your hands to mix thoroughly. Cover with plastic wrap, and leave in the fridge for around 1 hour. Remove the vegetables, drain any excess water and stir in the cornstarch.

Place a dumpling wrapper in your palm and put 2 generous teaspoons of the filling in the middle. Gently bring one half of the dumpling sheet over the other half and squeeze the edges. To make the dumpling more decorative, add some folds around the edges. Continue until the remaining 29 dumpling wrappers are filled.

Heat a wok over low heat, add the canola oil, and give it a swirl. Arrange the dumplings in the wok, cover (see tip), and cook for 2 minutes.

Put the flour in a jug, add around 9fl oz water, and mix until most lumps are gone. Pour over the frying dumplings, turn the heat to medium, cover with a lid, and cook until the water has evaporated.

Gently remove the dumplings from the wok (the flour-water will turn into a crispy and delicate flour sheet and may break easily when lifting the dumplings out from the pan).

Arrange on a serving plate and garnish each dumpling with 2 chives criss-crossed over the top.

Ching's Tip
A see-through lid is handy, so that you can see, without lifting the lid, when the water has evaporated.

VEGAN "TOM YUM" (SOUP)

10 mins

8 mins

Ve GF DF

1 tablespoon vegetable bouillon
   powder
1 garlic clove, grated
1 teaspoon grated *galangal*, or
   peeled and grated ginger
1 stalk of lemongrass, grated
1 kaffir lime leaf, fresh or dried
1 red chile, seeded and finely
   chopped
2oz fresh firm tofu, drained and
   sliced into ¾-inch cubes
4 fresh shiitake mushrooms,
   rinsed, and sliced
4 cherry tomatoes
½ head of baby bok choy, leaves
   separated
scant ½ cup reduced-fat
   coconut milk
pinch of soft brown sugar
1 tablespoon tamari or low-
   sodium light soy sauce
juice of 1 lime

To serve
small handful of Thai basil leaves,
   finely shredded
small handful of fresh cilantro,
   roughly chopped

A spicy Thai classic, to which I've added a few more ingredients, that is just bursting with flavor. The chile and ginger not only add wonderful spice notes, but also are thermogenic, meaning they speed up the metabolism. The tofu provides protein, iron, and calcium, and a host of minerals. Shiitake mushrooms are not only delicious, they're also a good source of iron and antioxidants, and boost the immune system. A tasty dish that is also fabulous for your health!

Serves 2 kcal 151 carbs 13g protein 8.9g fat 6.5g

Pour 2 cups water into a wok, and bring to a boil. Add the bouillon powder, and stir to dissolve, then add all the ingredients down to, and including the chile. Bring to a gentle simmer, and cook for 10 minutes until the broth is infused with their flavors.

Add the tofu and mushrooms, and cook for 3 minutes. Then add the tomatoes, and simmer for 1–2 minutes.

Reduce the heat to low, and add the bok choy, coconut milk, sugar, tamari or light soy sauce, and the lime juice. Season to taste to your liking adding more chiles, lime juice, or salt if you wish.

To serve, ladle the soup into two large bowls and garnish with the basil and cilantro.

10 mins

5 mins

Ve GF DF

VEGAN SMOKED TOFU AND HOT AND SOUR ZUCCHINI NOODLES

2 large zucchini, cut thinly
    lengthwise to make zucchini
    noodles
3 ½oz smoked tofu, cut into
    julienne strips

For the fragrant hot oil dressing
1 tablespoon canola oil
1 garlic clove, minced
1-inch piece of ginger, peeled and
    grated
1 red chile, seeded and finely
    chopped
1 tablespoon tamari or low-
    sodium light soy sauce
1 tablespoon Chinkiang black
    rice vinegar or balsamic
    vinegar
½ tablespoons toasted sesame
    oil
1 tablespoon Sichuan chili oil
pinch of ground toasted Sichuan
    peppercorns
pinch of cracked sea salt
small handful of chopped
    cilantro

A great low-carb dinner with a spicy kick! The zucchini noodles are full of fiber, the hot oil dressing is super tasty, and the black rice vinegar provides a nice tangy-sour flavor.

Serves 2 kcal 241 carbs 10.3g protein 14.9g fat 15.6g

Pour 2 cups water into a medium pan, and bring to a boil. Keep on a gentle simmer.

To make the dressing, heat a wok over high heat until smoking, add the canola oil, and give it a swirl. Add the garlic, ginger, and red chile, and toss for a few seconds, then add the rest of the ingredients. Set aside to keep hot.

Toss the zucchini strips into the simmering water, lift out, drain, and add to the wok together with the smoked tofu. Toss it all together well to heat through, then eat immediately.

SWEETCORN MAPO TOFU

1–2 tablespoons peanut oil

2 garlic cloves crushed, peeled and minced

1-inch piece ginger, peeled and grated

1 red chile, seeded and finely chopped

1 teaspoon fermented salted black beans, rinsed, crushed

1 tablespoon chili bean paste

1½ cups fresh corn kernels (from about 3 medium ears)

9oz firm fresh tofu, drained, sliced into 1-inch cubes

1 tablespoon Shaohsing rice wine or dry sherry

1 tablespoon tamari or low-sodium light soy sauce

1 tablespoon Chinkiang black rice or balsamic vinegar

7fl oz hot vegetable stock

1 tablespoon Sichuan preserved vegetables in chili oil, finely chopped

1 tablespoon cornstarch, blended with 2 tablespoons cold water

For the garnish

2 tablespoons chili oil

2 pinches of toasted ground Sichuan peppercorns

1 scallion, finely sliced

small handful of chopped cilantro stems, and hand-picked leaves

Spicy mapo tofu was invented by Mrs. Chen, a Sichuan street hawker who put the dish and Chengdu on the culinary map! The classic version includes some ground pork and Sichuan preserved vegetables, for that sour, briny taste, which I like, but I have substituted tofu for the pork and added some corn kernels for a sweet, modern vegan take! Serve with jasmine rice.

Serves 2 kcal 378 carbs 23.2g protein 17g fat 24.2g

Heat a wok over high heat, and add the peanut oil. Give it a swirl, and add the garlic, ginger, and chile. Cook, stirring, for a few seconds, then add the fermented salted black beans and the chili bean paste, followed by the corn kernels and tofu, and toss, cooking for 10 seconds.

Add the rice wine or dry sherry, tamari or soy sauce, vinegar, and stock, and bring to a boil. Stir in the Sichuan preserved vegetables and blended cornstarch.

Serve immediately with jasmine rice, garnished with the chili oil, ground toasted Sichuan peppercorns, scallion, and cilantro stems and leaves.

10 mins

5 mins

V DF

SICHUAN-STYLE LIANG MIAN

10½ oz dried egg noodles

1 tablespoon toasted sesame oil

For the hot sauce

1 tablespoon canola oil

2 cloves garlic, finely chopped

1-inch of ginger, peeled and grated

1 red chile, seeded and finely chopped

1 tablespoon chili bean paste

1 tablespoon shaohsing rice wine or dry sherry

2 tablespoons black sesame paste or tahini

¼ cup hot vegetable stock

2—3 tablespoons tamari or low-sodium light soy sauce

1 tablespoon black rice vinegar or balsamic vinegar

2 pinches of soft brown sugar

2 tablespoons toasted sesame oil

2 tablespoons chili oil

For the garnish

pinch of ground toasted Sichuan pepper

5oz bean sprouts, washed

3 scallions, sliced into julienne strips

1 large handful fresh cilantro

3 tablespoons toasted white sesame seeds

A delicious cold egg noodle salad, where the dressing is wokked up, and then assembled. The spicy Sichuan flavors are particularly refreshing on a hot summer's day. It can easily be doubled up for a family buffet too! For vegans, substitute the egg noodles with plain wheatflour noodles of your choice.

Serves 4 kcal 521 carbs 58.7g protein 13.9g fat 27.2g

Cook the noodles according to the package instructions, then drain, and refresh under cold water. Drain well, and season with a tablespoon of toasted sesame oil.

Heat a wok over high heat and add the canola oil, give it a swirl, then add the garlic, ginger and chile, and cook, stirring, for a few seconds. Add the chili bean paste, rice wine, sesame paste or tahini, vegetable stock, tamari or light soy sauce, rice vinegar, brown sugar, and sesame and chili oils. Stir well until well-combined. Remove from the heat and pour in the noodles. Tossing them well. Transfer to a serving plate.

Chill in the fridge for 20 minutes, then sprinkle over the ground Sichuan pepper.

Blanch the bean sprouts in hot water for 10 seconds, then drain and rinse in cold water.

Serve garnished with scallions, cilantro, bean sprouts and toasted white sesame seeds.

8 mins

4 mins

Ve GF DF

WOK FRIED GINGER MISO SPINACH

1 tablespoon peanut oil

1 pinch of sea salt

2 garlic cloves, peeled and crushed, left whole

14oz baby spinach leaves

For the ginger miso sauce

1-inch piece of ginger, peeled and grated

1 tablespoon organic red miso paste

1 tablespoon tamari or low-sodium light soy sauce

3 tablespoons hot water

1 tablespoon Shaohsing rice wine or dry sherry

pinch of superfine sugar

For the garnish

1–2 scallions, trimmed and finely sliced

2 teaspoons toasted sesame seeds

A simple vegan stir-fry of baby spinach leaves that are wilted and seasoned in a gingery miso sauce, making a deliciously addictive light supper served with rice.

Serves 2 kcal 122 carbs 3.6g protein 13.9g fat 27.2g

In a jug, whisk together the ingredients for the sauce and stir until well-combined.

Heat a wok over a high heat, and add the peanut oil. Give it a swirl, and add the salt to dissolve, then the garlic, stir for a few seconds, then add the spinach. Cook, tossing the spinach for a few seconds, and then add the sauce, and toss with the spinach. Cook the spinach down in the sauce to wilt it.

To serve, spoon some of the ginger miso spinach over jasmine rice, garnish with the scallions and toasted sesame seeds, and eat immediately.

30 mins

+ 3½ hours dough proving time

15 mins

Ve DF

MOCK DUCK BLACK PEPPER WITH BASIL SHEN JIAN BAO (STEAMED BUNS)

2¼ cups all-purpose flour

2 tablespoons superfine sugar

¼ teaspoon sea salt

1 teaspoon instant dry yeast

2 tablespoons canola oil

1-inch piece of ginger, peeled and grated

½ cup dried shiitake mushrooms, soaked in hot water for 20 minutes, drained and finely diced

½ tablespoon cornstarch blended with 2 tablespoons cold water

5oz Napa cabbage, finely chopped

½ tablespoon sesame oil

3oz mock duck, finely chopped

2 scallions, finely chopped

pinch of cracked black pepper

2 tablespoons vegetarian oyster sauce

2–3 tablespoons basil leaves, finely shredded

For the seasoning sauce

¼ teaspoon sea salt

½ vegetable stock cube, grated

¼ teaspoon sugar

¼ teaspoon ground white pepper

1 tablespoon tamari or low-sodium light soy sauce

contd overleaf

>

Although this isn't the quickest recipe in this book, it's worth the effort as it's super delicious, especially if you like a fluffy bao with a savory peppery filling. I've gone all vegan on this one, but you can use cooked meats if you prefer. The trick to achieving a golden pan-fried bottom and a moist soft top is to make sure your wok or saucepan has an even, flat bottom, and a tight-fitting lid with a hole that allows the steam to escape. Eat while they're still piping hot, and dunk them into some thick sweet soy sauce.

Makes 18 buns kcal 97 carbs 18.3g protein 2.6g fat 2g*

In a large bowl, mix the flour, sugar, salt, and yeast with ¾ cup lukewarm water. Knead the mixture for 10–12 minutes until elastic. Cover with a clean tea towel, and leave in a warm place for 3 hours to rise until it has doubled in size.

Punch the air out, and divide the dough into 18 small balls. Knead the balls individually, then cover, and leave in a warm place to rise for an additional 20 minutes.

Combine all the ingredients for the seasoning sauce.

Heat a wok over medium heat, add 1 tablespoon of canola oil, and give it a swirl. Fry the ginger for 30 seconds. Add the mushrooms and seasoning sauce, and stir-fry for 1 minute. Stir in the blended cornstarch and stir-fry for 1 minute, or until the sauce thickens. Add the Napa cabbage and sesame oil, and fry briefly to make sure all the ingredients are thoroughly mixed. Remove from the heat.

Add the mock duck and scallions into the cabbage mixture and mix well. Season further with the black pepper and vegetarian oyster sauce and toss in the shredded basil leaves.

To serve
small dish of thick soy sauce
small dish of sweet chili sauce
small dish equal amounts of
    vegetarian oyster sauce and
    sriracha chili sauce

*per bao

Flatten the dough balls. Using a rolling pin, roll over each flattened dough a few times. Then, taking the dough by the edge, gently go over the edge of the dough with the rolling pin. The aim is to try and achieve a round dough sheet of a thickness of around 3mm in the middle with a much thinner edge.

Taking a dough sheet in the palm of your hand, place a generous tablespoonful of the vegetable mixture in the middle. Then cup your palm so the filling remains in the middle of the dough sheet; gently gather the edge of the sheet into the middle and twist to seal the edge. It's a bit like making a *Xiao long bao*, except this time, the filling is concealed within the dough.

Continue until all the dough sheets are filled. Heat a wok over a low heat, add the remaining canola oil and give it a swirl. Arrange the filled dough buns around the pan (cook in two batches, depending on the size of your wok), leaving a 5mm space in between so the dough buns have enough space to rise during cooking. Cover and cook for 1–2 minutes, then add water to cover half of the filled buns and sprinkle some water over the top of the buns.

Turn the heat to medium, cover with a lid and cook until all the water has evaporated and the bottom of the buns has turned crispy and golden brown. Serve with a small dish each of thick soy sauce, sweet chili sauce and vegetarian oyster sauce mixed with sriracha chili sauce.

5 mins

2 mins

Ve GF DF

GARLIC WOK TOSSED BABY BOK CHOY

1 tablespoon canola oil

1 pinch of sea salt

2 garlic cloves, peeled, crushed finely chopped

7oz baby bok choy, washed, sliced in half down the length

1 tablespoon Shaosing rice wine or dry sherry

1 teaspoon toasted sesame oil

One of my favorite ways of serving bok choy, this is a deliciously crunchy side that is also incredibly quick and easy to make.

Serves 4 kcal 87 carbs 3.1g protein 1.7g fat 7.2g

Heat a wok over high heat, add the canola oil, give the oil a swirl and then add the sea salt and finely chopped garlic. Add the baby bok choy, toss wokking for 30 seconds. Add the Shaohsing rice wine or dry sherry and cook for another 30 seconds until the leaves have wilted but still aldente.

Season with sesame oil. Remove and serve.

20 mins

to cook the sushi rice
+ 20 minutes chill time
for the rice

5-6 mins

Ve GF DF

For the rice

9oz short-grain sushi rice,
   washed well and drained
½ teaspoon vegetable bouillon
   powder

For the vegetables

1 tablespoon peanut oil
½ tablespoon minced garlic
1 teaspoon seeded and finely
   chopped red chile
1 tablespoon finely chopped
   shallots
3½oz fresh corn kernels (about 1
   medium ear)
generous 3oz baby asparagus,
   sliced into ⅜-inch rounds
2½oz fresh shiitake mushrooms,
   stalks removed, diced
3 tablespoons tamari or low-
   sodium light soy sauce
1 tablespoon Shaohsing rice wine
   or dry sherry
1 teaspoon toasted sesame oil
2 pinches of ground white
   pepper
To serve (optional)
2 large eggs
1 tablespoon peanut oil

For the garnish

4 x 2 ¾ x 1½ pieces of roasted
   seaweed, torn into 1-inch
   pieces
½ teaspoon Japanese *Togarashi*
   dried chile peppers

VEGGIE SEAWEED ASPARAGUS FRIED RICE WITH OPTIONAL FRIED EGGS

The corn, asparagus, and roasted seaweed add a delicious sweet and umami flavor to this dish, and sushi rice, as an alternative to the usual jasmine rice, gives a slightly sticky and satisfying starchiness (in a good way). Non-vegans can top with two fried runny eggs, if they like.

Serves 2 kcal 719 carbs 116.2g protein 22.3g fat 21.4g

Place the drained rice in a medium pan, stir in the vegetable bouillon powder and 15fl oz water and bring to a boil. Turn the heat to low, cover the pan, and cook for 15 minutes. Remove the lid, fluff up the rice, and spread out on a tray, then leave to cool at room temperature for 15—20 minutes.

Heat a wok over high heat until smoking, add the peanut oil, and give it a swirl. Add the garlic, chile, and shallots, and stir for a few seconds to release their aroma. Add the corn, and wok-fry for 10 seconds, then add the asparagus and wok-fry for a further few seconds. Add the mushrooms, and cook for 1 minute. Season with 1 tablespoon of the tamari or light soy sauce and the rice wine or dry sherry.

Push the vegetables to the side of the wok, add the rice, and toss, cooking until all the ingredients are well-combined. Season with the remaining tamari or light soy sauce, the sesame oil, and white pepper.

Remove the fried rice and place in two clay pots. Put the lids on and keep the rice warm in a slow oven while you cook the eggs, if you're serving these.

When ready to serve, fry the eggs in the oil sunny-side up until crispy on the bottom. Top each portion of rice with an egg, and sprinkle each with half the seaweed and *Togarashi* chile pepper.

FISH &

SHELLFISH

5 mins

5–8 mins

GF DF

TAIWANESE-STYLE SEAFOOD "PANCAKE"

¼ cup potato flour

6 ½ tablespoons cornstarch

2 scallions, finely diced

1 red chile, seeded and finely diced

2 tablespoons canola oil

3 ½oz fresh mixed seafood (squid rings, mussels, and tiger shrimp)

2 eggs

3oz bok choy, each leaf sliced down the stalk into ¼-inch strips

sliced scallions, to garnish

For the sweet hot sauce

2 tablespoons hoisin sauce

2 tablespoons oyster sauce

2 teaspoons sriracha chili sauce

This delicious snack or quick mid-week supper is inspired by my love of the oyster omelets that you get in the street food stalls found in the night markets in Taiwan. It involves making a thin, egg crêpe-like pancake. The trick is to stir-fry the seafood first, and then pour in the potato and cornstarch batter and cook it like a thin, eggy crêpe. Serve it with a spicy, sweet concoction of hoisin, oyster and sriracha sauces—so umami and full of yum!

If you're vegan, you can use an assortment of sliced fresh shiitake, shimeji, and enoki mushrooms instead of the seafood.

Serves 2 kcal 415 carbs 48g protein 17.6g fat 17.4g

Combine all the ingredients for the sweet hot sauce in a bowl and set aside.

Mix the potato flour and cornstarch in a generous ⅓ cup cold water, then add the diced scallions and chile.

Heat a wok over medium heat, add 1 tablespoon of the canola oil, and give the oil a swirl. Add half the mixed seafood, and fry for a few seconds, then add half the scallions and chile starch mixture. Lightly beat one of the eggs and add to the wok with half the bok choy.

Cook for 2–3 minutes until the potato flour mixture has turned a translucent color. Spoon out onto a serving plate, and cover with foil to keep it warm. Make the second "pancake" in the same way, using the remaining ingredients.

To serve, drizzle with the sweet hot sauce, and garnish with some sliced scallions.

20 mins

5 mins

DF

OYSTER SAUCE, MISO, AND HONEY SPICED SHRIMP CHOW MEIN

For the marinade

1 tablespoon peeled and freshly grated ginger

1 tablespoon organic miso paste

2 tablespoons oyster sauce

1 teaspoon dark soy sauce

1 tablespoon all-purpose flour

For the stir-fry

12 large raw tiger shrimp, tail on, shelled and deveined

2 tablespoons canola oil

1 garlic clove, peeled, and crushed, left whole

1 red chile, seeded and finely chopped

1 tablespoon Shaohsing rice wine or dry sherry

2 tablespoons runny honey

2 tablespoons tamari or low-sodium light soy sauce

1 teaspoon chili oil

12oz cooked egg noodles, seasoned with toasted sesame oil

For the garnish

1 large handful bean sprouts

2 scallions, sliced into rings on the diagonal

An all-around Asian fusion dish that is salty, spicy, and sweet. The miso, oyster sauce, and honey work particularly well with the sweetness of the shrimp. It's perfect with cooked egg noodles tossed through.

Serves 2   kcal 534   carbs 83.4g   protein 21.2g   fat 15.2g

Combine all the ingredients for the marinade in a bowl and mix well to form a paste. Add the shrimp, toss to coat and leave to marinate for 15 minutes.

Heat a wok or pan over a high heat, and add the canola oil. Give it a swirl, then add the garlic and chile, and cook, stirring, for a few seconds to release their aroma. Add the marinated shrimp, and cook, tossing for 1 minute. Season with the rice wine, honey, tamari or light soy sauce and chili oil, and coat well. Continue to cook, tossing, to caramelize the shrimp for another minute until they have turned pink. Add the noodles and toss through to mix well.

Serve immediately, garnished with the bean sprouts and scallions.

15 mins

10 mins

GF **DF**

CRISPY "FAMILY SNAPPER" WITH BLACK BEAN SAUCE

For the black bean sauce

2oz fermented salted black beans

1 tablespoon Shaohsing rice wine or dry sherry

1 tablespoon peanut oil

2 tablespoons peeled and grated garlic

2 tablespoons peeled and freshly grated ginger

1 red chile, seeded and finely chopped

9fl oz chicken or vegetable stock

1 teaspoon tamari or low-sodium light soy sauce

pinch of ground white pepper, or to taste

1 tablespoon cornstarch, blended with 2 tablespoons cold water

For the snapper

1 x 18oz whole red snapper, cleaned and scaled

2/3 cup potato flour

coarse salt, to taste

1–2 teaspoons ground white pepper, or to taste

vegetable oil, for deep-frying

For the garnish

edible flowers

1–2 scallions, cut into julienne strips

Perfect for a Chinese New Year Party, this spectacular dish is very easy to make. If you prefer, you could use chunks of cod and serve it in a fish-shaped platter—the skeleton is really just for an "X-factor" presentation. Serve with jasmine rice and steamed greens.

Serves 4 kcal 220 carbs 25.8g protein 17.6g fat 5.3g

To make the sauce, soak the beans in cold water for a few minutes to remove the salt. Drain, and pour over the rice wine or dry sherry, then use a fork or the back of a spoon to mash them.

Heat a wok over high heat until smoking, add the oil, and give it a swirl. Add the garlic, ginger and chile, and stir-fry briefly until just beginning to brown and catch on the wok. Add the beans, stir briefly, and then add the stock, tamari or light soy sauce, and white pepper. Bring to a boil, stirring, add the blended cornstarch, and cook until the sauce thickens and is glistening.

Fillet the fish, keeping the skeleton whole with the head intact. Cut the fish into 2-inch cubes. Mix together the potato flour, salt and white pepper, and lightly dust the skeleton and head. Toss the fish pieces in the flour mixture until well-coated, then shake off the excess.

Heat about 3 inches of vegetable oil in a deep-fryer or a wok to 350°F. Using two metal skewers, pierce the fish skeleton in two spots to secure it in a slightly curved shape. Gently lower the skeleton into the oil and fry briefly on both sides until light golden. Drain on paper towels, and set aside. When ready to serve, fry the fish quickly, until cooked through, and just beginning to turn light golden, 1–2 minutes.

Arrange the fish skeleton, standing upright, on a serving platter and pile the fish pieces either side. You can pour the hot black bean sauce over the fish, and place the rest in a gravy boat for guests to pour over rice. Garnish with edible flowers and the scallion strips, and serve.

SHRIMP "BAN" MEIN

10 mins

6 mins

DF

For the noodles

9oz dried wheat flour noodles

1 tablespoon toasted sesame oil

For the stir-fry

2 tablespoons peanut oil

½ teaspoon ground dry-toasted Sichuan peppercorns

2 red chiles, seeded and finely chopped

2 scallions, finely chopped

9oz raw tiger shrimp, shelled with heads off, tail on, deveined

3 ½oz bean sprouts

small handful of cilantro

For the sauce

scant ½ cup cold vegetable stock

2 tablespoons tamari or low-sodium light soy sauce

1 tablespoon toasted sesame oil

1 tablespoon Chinkiang black rice vinegar or balsamic vinegar

1 teaspoon chili oil

1 tablespoon cornstarch blended with 2 tablespoons cold water

Both a "ban mein" and a "chow mein" contain stir-fried shrimp, but a "ban mein" is saucy, rather than dry. This woks in less than 6 minutes, and makes great use of your pantry ingredients. I've used bean sprouts for their satisfying crunch, but you could use any seasonal vegetables of your choice. It's such a versatile dish, you'll make it time and time again.

Serves 2 kcal 825 carbs 102.9g protein 40.3g fat 27g

Put all the sauce ingredients in a jug and mix well.

Cook the noodles according to package instructions, and drain well. Drizzle with the sesame oil to prevent them from sticking together.

Heat a wok over high heat until smoking, add the peanut oil, and give the oil a swirl. Add the ground Sichuan peppercorns, red chiles, and scallions, and toss for a few seconds. Add the shrimp, and cook for 1 minute. Pour in the sauce, and bring to a boil, then add the cooked noodles, and toss together well to coat in the sauce. Add the bean sprouts, and give it all one last toss, then sprinkle the cilantro on top and serve immediately.

YU SIANG HALIBUT

15 mins

10 mins

GF DF

14oz whole halibut fillets, skinned
pinch of sea salt
pinch of ground white pepper
1 tablespoon Shaohsing rice wine
   or dry sherry
1 teaspoon cornstarch, blended
   with 1 tablespoon cold water
2 tablespoons canola oil
2 garlic cloves, minced
1-inch piece of ginger, peeled and
   finely grated
1 red chile, seeded and finely
   chopped
1 scallion, finely sliced

For the sauce
1 tablespoon chili bean paste
scant ½ cup cold vegetable
   stock
1 tablespoon tamari or low-
   sodium light soy sauce
1 tablespoon Chinkiang black
   rice vinegar or balsamic
   vinegar
1 tablespoon cornstarch blended
   with 2 tablespoons cold water

For the garnish
1 scallion, sliced into strips and
   soaked in iced water for 5
   minutes to curl, then drained
cilantro leaves

When I was working with Ken Hom on the television series "Exploring China", we filmed with the famous chef, Yu Bo, who made us his spectacular *yu siang* shrimp dish. *Yu siang* was originally a dish of braised pork and eggplant, but translates as "'fish fragrant". Some Sichuan chefs contend that fish sauce was used in the original sauce, hence the name, but we may never know the answer to this conundrum. In any case, I'm making it here with meaty halibut. It's quick, easy, and delicious, and for once *yu siang* sauce is actually appropriate!

Serves 2 kcal 366 carbs 17.2g protein 41g fat 15g

Place the fish fillets on a deep, heatproof serving plate. Season with the sea salt, white pepper, rice wine or dry sherry, and the blended cornstarch.

Set the plate on a stainless steel rack over a wok filled with water. Place the lid on, and steam the fish over medium heat for 8 minutes.

Meanwhile, combine all the ingredients for the sauce in a bowl and mix well.

Heat another wok over high heat until smoking, add the canola oil, and swirl it around. Wok-fry the garlic, ginger, chile, and scallion for a few seconds, then add the sauce, and bring to a boil, then set over very low heat.

Remove the fish from the steamer to serving plates, and pour any juices collected into the wok, then mix well using a whisk, so the sauce is smooth. Pour the sauce over the fish, garnish with the scallion curls and cilantro leaves, and serve immediately with jasmine rice.

10 mins

8 mins

GF DF

STEAMED HADDOCK FILLETS WITH WOK-FRIED BACON

11oz haddock fillets, skinned and cut into 1-inch chunks
pinch of salt
pinch of ground white pepper
1 tablespoon cornstarch, blended with 2 tablespoons cold water
1 tablespoon peeled and freshly grated ginger
1 scallion, sliced into strips and soaked in iced water for 5 minutes to curl then drained, to garnish

For the wok-fry
1 tablespoon canola oil
1 teaspoon ground Sichuan peppercorns
2 dried red chiles
1 teaspoon peeled and freshly grated ginger
5oz smoked thick-cut bacon, cubed
½ teaspoon ground turmeric
1 tablespoon Shaohsing rice wine or dry sherry
1 teaspoon dark soy sauce
1 tablespoon tamari or low-sodium light soy sauce
juice of ½ lemon or 1 tablespoon Chinkiang black rice vinegar or balsamic vinegar
2 teaspoons chili oil

I have become a huge fan of wok-steaming fish for a quick, healthy supper. Haddock fillets have a firm, flaky texture when cooked, and are delish with wokked-up spicy thick-cut bacon, diced on top. Perfect served with some blanched or steamed greens and jasmine rice.

Serves 2 kcal 445 carbs 13.7g protein 41.9g fat 25.6g

Place the haddock on a heatproof serving plate and season with the salt, white pepper, and blended cornstarch, then cover with the grated ginger.

Set the plate on a steamer rack set over a wok filled with water. Place the lid on, and steam the haddock over medium-high heat for 6 minutes.

Meanwhile, heat another wok over high heat until smoking, add the canola oil and give it a swirl. Add the Sichuan peppercorns, dried chiles, and ginger, and stir for a few seconds to release their aroma. Add the diced thick-cut bacon and turmeric, and wok-fry for a few seconds, then season with the rice wine or dry sherry, the dark soy sauce, tamari or light soy sauce, lemon juice or vinegar, and the chili oil.

Remove the fish from the steamer to serving plates. Spoon the wok-fried diced thick-cut bacon on top, then garnish with the scallion curls. Set on the table with some blanched or steamed greens, and serve with jasmine rice.

5 mins

12 mins

GF DF

THAI COCONUT COD CURRY

18oz cod loin, skinned, boned, and sliced into 1-inch chunks
pinch of salt
pinch of ground white pepper
2 tablespoons Thai red curry paste, plus 1 teaspoon
1 tablespoon cornstarch, blended with 2 tablespoons cold water
2 tablespoons canola oil
2 baby shallots, sliced, or ½ white onion, diced
1 stalk of lemongrass, any tough outer leaves discarded, sliced on the diagonal into 1½-inch lengths
7fl oz coconut milk
scant ½ cup cold vegetable stock
1 tablespoon fish sauce
3½ oz snow peas

For the garnish
Thai basil leaves
1 red chile, sliced, seeds in

When I need a warming curry, I instinctively go for this super delicious, quick and easy wok dish that can be on the table in less than 20 minutes. All you have to do is arm yourself with some cod, shallots, snow peas, and red chiles, and some pantry staples like coconut milk, fish sauce, and Thai red curry paste, and the rest is easy.

If you're vegan, substitute fried tofu chunks and oyster mushrooms for the cod.

Serves 2 kcal 406 carbs 20.4g protein 47.6g fat 13.4g

Season the cod with salt and ground white pepper. Using a brush, brush 1 teaspoon of the Thai red curry paste onto the fish, then pour the blended cornstarch over the fish.

Heat a wok over medium heat, add 1 tablespoon of the canola oil, and give the oil a swirl. Add the shallots or onions and lemongrass, and stir-fry for a few seconds to release their aroma.

Add the 2 tablespoons of Thai red curry paste and stir around to distribute in the wok. Add the remaining canola oil and the marinated cod and sear the fish for a few seconds. Pour in a little water around the edges of the wok to help create some steam, then add the coconut milk and stock. Bring to the boil, and gently poach the cod for about 5 minutes, until it has turned opaque white.

Season with the fish sauce, then add the snow peas, and cook for 30 seconds. Spoon out, garnish with the Thai basil and sliced red chile, and serve with jasmine rice.

20 mins

+ 15 minutes to
cook the rice

3 mins

DF

KIRAKUYA FIREBALLS

4oz fresh tuna or salmon, or
    sushi-grade smoked salmon,
    diced
3 tablespoons mayonnaise
2 tablespoons sake
1 teaspoon sriracha chili sauce
1 teaspoon finely sliced cilantro
    stems
1 scant cup cooked sushi rice
1 tablespoon seasoned sushi rice
    vinegar
1 teaspoon superfine sugar
1 large egg, beaten
4½oz panko bread crumbs
vegetable oil, for deep-frying

For the sake-soy dipping sauce
6 tablespoons sake
4 tablespoons tamari or low-
    sodium light soy sauce
juice of ½ lemon
1 tablespoon sugar

For the wasabi mayonnaise
4 tablespoons mayonnaise
4 teaspoons wasabi paste

*per fireball

This memorable dish is one I created for Kirakuya, a Japanese
sake bar in midtown Manhattan, when I was filming *Restaurant
Redemption* back in 2014. It went down a storm. I called them
fireballs because they are full of flavor and heat! They consist
of hot fish encased in sushi rice, and covered in panko bread
crumbs. Deep-fried until golden, they're served with a boozy
sake-soy dipping sauce and/or wasabi mayonnaise.

Makes 8 kcal 160 carbs 15g protein 6.7g fat 8.1g*

Combine all the ingredients for the sake-soy dipping sauce in a
small bowl and stir until the sugar is dissolved.

To make the wasabi mayonnaise, combine the mayonnaise and
wasabi paste in another small bowl.

In a mixing bowl, combine the diced tuna or salmon or smoked
salmon, the mayonnaise, sake, sriracha chili sauce, and cilantro.

Lay the cooked sushi rice flat out on a baking sheet. In a
small bowl, mix the seasoned rice vinegar with the sugar until
dissolved, then drizzle over the cooked sushi rice.

Using a small scoop or measuring spoon, scoop a 2 tablespoon-
portion of rice and form into a rough ball. Press a hole into the
center of the rice ball and stuff with 1 tablespoon of the fish
mixture. Press the opening closed and roll the ball between
your hands to reform. Repeat until all the fish mixture and rice
are used.

Place the beaten egg in a small bowl and the panko bread
crumbs in a shallow dish or on a pie plate.

Roll the fish rice balls in the beaten egg, and then into the bread
crumbs to coat.

Add enough oil to a wok for deep-frying, and heat to 350°F.
Deep-fry the rice balls for 2–3 minutes until golden brown. Drain
on paper towels. Serve immediately with the sake-soy dipping
sauce and wasabi mayonnaise.

15 mins

10 mins

GF DF

CHING'S FISH BALL NOODLE SOUP

For the fish balls
7oz whole haddock fillets, skinned, and finely chopped
2oz squid, cleaned
pinch of sea salt flakes
pinch of ground white pepper
1 teaspoon Shaohsing rice wine or dry sherry
1 tablespoon cornstarch
1 large egg white
1 teaspoon oyster sauce
1 tablespoon finely sliced cilantro stems

For the broth
1½ quarts fresh fish stock
7oz Napa cabbage, cut into 1-inch slices
7oz (about 4 cups) cooked vermicelli rice noodles
pinch of sea salt flakes
pinch of ground white pepper
1 tablespoon tamari or low-sodium light soy sauce
1 teaspoon toasted sesame oil

To serve
1 teaspoon chili oil, or to taste
cilantro leaves
1 tablespoon finely chopped chives

Ever since I tried my first steaming bowl of fish ball noodle soup in Hong Kong, I have been obsessed with it. The balls have a delicious "chew" to them—spongy in a fishy, delicate way—and they're served in an addictive, oniony broth, with clear rice noodles and umami seaweed. I like the soup laden with lots of a lip-smackingly hot chili oil—you get my point.

This is my version, and it doesn't disappoint; the trick is to add squid, which hardens when cooked, and gives the fish more of a satisfying "chew". I reckon my homemade fishballs are even better than some manufactured ones, which contain too much starch, and not enough fish. I hope you enjoy them.

Serves 2 kcal 327 carbs 36.2g protein 29.2g fat 8.4g

Place the haddock and squid in a food processor, season with the salt, white pepper, rice wine or dry sherry, the cornstarch, egg white, and oyster sauce, and blend well until airy and light. Sprinkle in the cilantro stems, and mix well. Using 2 tablespoons, pass some of the fish mixture from spoon to spoon, turning the mixture until an oval ball (quenelle) is formed—you should get 12 balls.

Add the fish stock to a large wok, and bring to a simmer. Add the Napa cabbage, and cook for 1 minute. Add the cooked noodles, and season with sea salt and white pepper.

Turn the heat to medium, and gently add the fish balls to the wok. Cook for 2–3 minutes until the fish balls float to the surface and turn opaque white.

Season with the tamari or light soy sauce and sesame oil.

Divide the noodles between two bowls, ladle in the stock and cabbage, and place six fish balls into each bowl. Drizzle with the chili oil, sprinkle over the cilantro leaves and chives, and serve immediately.

20 mins

4 mins

GF DF

BANG BANG CHILI BEAN SHRIMP NOODLE SALAD

This is my take on the Sichuan bang bang chicken noodle salad. Quick and easy, it's low in calories too! The shrimp are wok-fried in chili bean paste, black rice vinegar and soy, then served while they are still hot on the cold noodle salad. I love the bit of ying and yang that this dish brings.

If you are vegan, use shimeji mushrooms instead of the shrimp.

Serves 2 kcal 611 carbs 52.3g protein 14.6g fat 38.8g

For the shrimp

1 tablespoon canola oil

10 large raw tiger shrimp, shelled and deveined

1 teaspoon chili bean paste

1 teaspoon black rice vinegar

1 teaspoon tamari or low-sodium light soy sauce

For the noodles

3¹/₂oz dried vermicelli mung bean noodles, soaked in hot water for 5—6 minutes

¹/₂ cucumber, seeded and sliced into long julienne strips

1¹/₂oz radish, thinly sliced

1¹/₂oz carrot, sliced into long julienne strips

1 red chile, seeded and finely chopped

1 large scallion, finely sliced

toasted mixed black and white sesame seeds, to sprinkle

For the dressing

2 tablespoons canola oil

1 tablespoon grated ginger root

1 tablespoon toasted sesame oil

2 tablespoons sesame paste

1 tablespoon crunchy peanut butter

1 tablespoon tamari or low-sodium light soy sauce

2 tablespoons black rice vinegar

¹/₂ teaspoon dried red pepper flakes

¹/₂ teaspoon ground Sichuan peppercorns

Place all the dressing ingredients in a bowl, and whisk well to combine to a smooth dressing.

Arrange the drained noodles on two serving plates. Layer the cucumber, radish, carrot, red chile, and scallion on top. Cover with plastic wrap, and chill in the fridge until ready to serve.

Heat a wok over high heat until smoking, add the canola oil, and give the oil a swirl. Add the tiger shrimp, chili bean paste, vinegar, and tamari or light soy sauce, and toss for 1 minute until the shrimp have all turned pink and are cooked through.

To serve, remove the noodle salad from the fridge, place the hot spiced shrimp on top, and sprinkle with some toasted sesame seeds. Spoon some of the dressing over, and serve immediately, with the remaining dressing on the side.

GOLDEN MACANESE COD

20 mins

6–7 mins

GF DF

26 ½ oz cod loin, cut into 1-inch
    chunks
pinch of sea salt
pinch of ground white pepper
1 tablespoon cornstarch,
    blended with 2 tablespoons
    cold water
2 tablespoons canola oil
2 garlic cloves, finely chopped
2 shallots, finely chopped
½ teaspoon ground turmeric
1 teaspoon shrimp paste
2 generous cups vegetable stock
scant ½ cup coconut milk
1 tablespoon tamari or low-
    sodium light soy sauce
    (optional)

For the garnish
Thai basil
finely sliced deseeded red chiles

For the seasonal salad (optional)
7oz baby spinach leaves
3½oz snow peas
3½oz cherry tomatoes
1 red onion, diced
1 tablespoon extra virgin olive oil
juice of 1 lemon
pinch of sea salt
pinch of cracked black pepper

This dish is inspired by Macanese golden cod, but I'm using fresh cod instead of dried (bacalhau) and I also add vegetable stock and shrimp paste to give more sauce, as well as a deeper savory umami flavor. Serve with jasmine rice and a large seasonal salad.

If you are vegan, use zucchinis instead of the cod, and a vegetable bouillon stock cube instead of the shrimp paste.

Serves 4 kcal 304 carbs 16.4g protein 37.3g fat 10.6g

Place the cod in a bowl, and season with the sea salt and white pepper. Add the blended cornstarch, and toss the fish to coat well, then set aside.

Heat a wok over medium heat, add 1 tablespoon of the canola oil, and give it a swirl. Add the garlic and shallots, and fry for about 30 seconds until translucent and caramelized at the edges. Add the turmeric and shrimp paste, and stir for a few seconds, then add the remaining canola oil, and quickly add the cod. Sear the fish on one side and then, using a spatula, gently turn the pieces to sear on the other side. Pour in the vegetable stock and coconut milk, and bring to a boil, then cook over medium heat for about 4 minutes, until the liquid turns a deeper yellow in color, and the cod turns an opaque white and is cooked. Adjust the seasoning to taste with the tamari or light soy sauce, if you like.

Garnish with Thai basil and sliced red chiles, and serve immediately with a seasonal salad (simply toss all the salad ingredients together), if you like, and jasmine rice.

MACANESE-STYLE COD FISH AND POTATO BALLS

13oz cod loins, cut into 1-inch chunks
18oz baby potatoes, scrubbed
1 tablespoon canola oil
2 garlic cloves, minced
1 shallot, minced
½ teaspoon turmeric
1 teaspoon shrimp paste
scant ½ cup coconut milk
2 tablespoons vegetable stock
scant 1 cup peanut or vegetable oil, for deep-frying

For the marinade
pinch of sea salt
pinch of ground white pepper
1 tablespoon cornstarch, blended with 2 tablespoons cold water

For the seasoning mix
1 stalk of lemongrass, grated
½ red cayenne chile pepper, seeded and finely diced
2 scallions, finely diced
5 sprigs of cilantro, leaves and stems finely chopped
2 pinches of sea salt
2 pinches of ground white pepper

For the coating
¾ cup all-purpose flour
5 eggs, lightly beaten
4⅔ cups panko bread crumbs

*per fish and potato ball

These are my take on Macanese fish and potato balls. The beauty of the dish is that you can make them in advance, freeze them, and then bake from frozen. Perfect served with a zesty red cabbage and tomato salad, with a lemon, soy, olive oil, salt and black pepper dressing.

Makes 12 kcal 225 carbs 26.4g protein 11.9g fat 8.4g*

Combine all the ingredients for the marinade in a bowl and mix well to form a paste. Add the cod and toss to coat.

Bring 1½ quarts of water to a boil in a medium pan. Add the potatoes, and cook for 20 minutes. Drain, and, using a fork, mash.

Heat a wok over medium heat, add the canola oil, and swirl in the pan. Add the garlic and shallot, and fry for about 30 seconds, until translucent and caramelized at the edges. Add the turmeric, shrimp paste, and cod. Sear the cod on one side, and then, using a spatula, gently turn the pieces and sear on the other side. Pour in the coconut milk and stock, bring to a boil, then cook until the liquid turns a deeper yellow in color. Remove the cod from the wok, and flake using a fork.

Combine the ingredients for the seasoning mix. Add to the mashed potatoes, flaked fish and half of the poaching liquid from the wok, being careful not to break up the fish pieces too much as you want some texture.

Place the flour, eggs, and bread crumbs in three separate bowls. Take 2 large tablespoons of the filling, shape into a ball with a diameter of about 1½ inches, dip into the flour, then the egg, and then the bread crumbs to coat. Double coat by repeating the process, and then continue until you have 12 balls.

Heat the peanut or vegetable oil in another wok to 350°F, or until a piece of bread turns golden in 15 seconds and floats to the surface. Lower each ball into the oil, one at a time, then, using a ladle, spoon the hot oil over to coat the ball. Fry for about 1 minute until golden and crisp. Remove, and place on a plate lined with paper towels. Serve with a fresh seasonal salad.

10 mins

3 mins

GF DF

SMOKIN' HOT SCALLOPS AND CHINESE CHIVES

2 tablespoons canola oil

1 tablespoon peeled and freshly grated ginger

1 small fresh habañero chile, seeded and finely chopped

2 small dried red chiles

8 large sea scallops, cleaned

bunch of Chinese chives, sliced into 1-inch pieces

1 tablespoon Shaohsing rice wine or vegetable stock

1 tablespoon tamari or low-sodium light soy sauce

1 tablespoon Chinkiang black rice vinegar or balsamic vinegar

1 teaspoon soft brown sugar

dash of toasted sesame oil

I am a sucker for the sweetness of scallops and the heat of chiles, and when you pair them with aromatic and pungent Chinese chives, you have a match made in culinary heaven. Delicious with jasmine rice and a glass of dry white wine.

Serves 2 kcal 200 carbs 8.4g protein 12.3g fat 13.3g

Heat a wok over high heat until smoking, add the canola oil, and give it a swirl. Add the ginger, fresh and dried chiles, and toss for a few seconds. Add the scallops and cook, tossing continuously, for 15 seconds–1 minute (depending on the size of the scallops). Add the chives and stir-fry for 1 minute, then season the mixture with the rice wine or vegetable stock, soy sauce, vinegar, sugar, and sesame oil. Toss until well combined and hot.

Transfer to serving plates, and serve immediately with steamed jasmine rice.

15 mins

5 mins

DF

GOLDEN SESAME SHRIMP BALLS

12oz raw tiger shrimp, shelled and deveined, 7oz ground in a food processor, 5oz cut into ¼-inch dice

2 cups sunflower or vegetable oil, for deep-frying

For the seasoning mix

1-inch piece of ginger, peeled and grated

1 large scallion, finely chopped

1 red chile, seeded and finely chopped

1 teaspoon Shaohsing rice wine or dry sherry

1 teaspoon tamari or low-sodium light soy sauce

1 large egg white, beaten

1 teaspoon toasted sesame oil

2 tablespoons cornstarch

pinch of cracked sea salt

pinch of ground black pepper

For the coating

¾ cup all-purpose flour

2 large egg yolks, beaten

¾ cup white sesame seeds

For the garnish and salad

cilantro leaves

mint leaves

1 red chile, seeded and finely chopped

2 heads Belgian endive, leaves separated, dressed with sweet chili sauce and lime juice (optional)

Shrimp toast is a firm favorite with my family, but one year I decided instead to make Golden Sesame Shrimp Balls—similar to the toast, except without the bread. The results were delicious. The trick is to get a ground, but chunky consistency, so there is a bite to them, and they hold their shape when fried. Delicious and so simple, they make a fab appetizer served with a Belgian endive salad dressed with sweet chili sauce, and a drizzle of lime juice.

Makes 10–12 kcal 147 carbs 10.4g protein 8.2g fat 8.4g*

Put all the ingredients for the seasoning mix into a medium bowl, and stir well with a fork to combine. Add the ground and diced shrimp to the bowl, and mix well to combine. Roll into 10–12 mini ping-pong-sized balls, and transfer to a plate.

Place the flour, egg yolks and sesame seeds in three separate bowls. Dip each shrimp ball first into the flour, then in the beaten egg yolks, and then into the sesame seeds. Set aside.

Heat the sunflower or vegetable oil in a wok over medium-high heat to 325°F, or until a bread cube dropped in the oil turns golden brown in 15 seconds, and floats to the surface. Using a strainer, lower the shrimp balls, one at a time, into the oil, and cook, tossing gently, for about 2 minutes, until golden brown. Drain on paper towels, and repeat with the remaining balls.

To serve, place the shrimp balls on a serving plate, and garnish with a sprinkling of cilantro leaves, mint leaves, and the chopped red chile. Or serve as a warm salad, if you like, with Belgian endive leaves dressed with sweet chili sauce and a drizzle of lime juice. Serve immediately.

*per shrimp ball

CHUNKY COD LAKSA

20 mins

30 mins

DF

9oz dried egg noodles
1 tablespoon canola oil
14fl oz coconut milk
2 cups vegetable or fish stock
juice of 1 lime
1 teaspoon soft brown sugar
1 teaspoon fish sauce
7oz cod loins, cut into 1-inch
    chunks, or raw shrimp, shelled
    with tails on, deveined
3oz bean sprouts
pinch of sea salt
pinch of ground dried red
    pepper flakes
small handful of cilantro leaves

For the laksa paste
1 teaspoon ground coriander
1 teaspoon ground cumin
1 teaspoon ground turmeric
½ onion, chopped
3 tablespoons coconut milk
1 tablespoon peeled and grated
    ginger or galangal
2 garlic cloves, crushed
1 stalk lemongrass, roughly
    chopped
1 red cayenne chile pepper,
    seeded, and roughly chopped
1 tablespoon shrimp paste

Laksa is a Malaysian—Chinese curry noodle broth. The spices used traveled from India, and the egg noodles came from southern China. It's easy to make your own laksa paste—just blend all the ingredients in a food processor. Then cook up with coconut milk and stock, and add cod, crunchy vegetables, such as bean sprouts, and fresh herbs, such as cilantro, for a fabulously spicy, delicious meal. Enjoy!

Serves 4 kcal 496 carbs 55.1g protein 19.8g fat 24g

Put all the ingredients for the laksa paste into a blender or food processor, and whizz to a smooth paste.

Meanwhile, cook the noodles in a pan of boiling water for about 3 minutes, then drain under running cold water to get rid of the starch, and help keep the noodles springy.

Heat the oil in a wok, and cook the laksa paste for a 1 minute.

Stir in the coconut milk, stock, lime juice, sugar, and fish sauce, then bring the soup to a boil and simmer for 20 minutes.

Add the cod or shrimps to the soup, and simmer until the fish changes color becomes opaque and is cooked through.

Add the bean sprouts, salt, and red pepper flakes to taste.

Divide the noodles evenly between serving bowls, and ladle the soup over. Garnish with cilantro leaves, and serve immediately.

10 mins

5 mins

GF DF

MY MOM'S SRIRACHA KETCHUP SHRIMP

1 tablespoon canola oil
10 large raw tiger shrimp,
    heads off, shells and tails on,
    deveined
4 tablespoons tomato ketchup
1 teaspoon sriracha chili sauce
1 tablespoon tamari or low-
    sodium light soy sauce
small bunch of chives, finely
    chopped, to garnish
lime wedges, to serve

This is an update on my mom's ketchup shrimp recipe. It sounds so wrong but it's actually so yum. She would sometimes add rice and turn it into a seafood ketchup fried rice. The trick is a good ketchup and to also add a splash of soy sauce to give an umaminess to the dish. I have also added a small dash of sriracha chili sauce to the dish, and with that small, but powerful update, the result is a tart, sweet, savory hot dish. Perfect with jasmine rice and some steamed vegetables. I urge you to wok on and try it!

Serves 2 kcal 124 carbs 6.4g protein 19g fat 23g

Heat a wok over high heat until smoking, add the canola oil, and give it a swirl. Add the tiger shrimp, and stir-fry until pink. Add the ketchup, sriracha, and soy sauce, and toss, cooking until the sauce has reduced and caramelized.

Garnish with the chives, squeeze some lime juice over, and serve immediately with jasmine rice and steamed greens.

5 mins

3 mins

GF DF

DRUNKEN SCALLOPS WITH SAMPHIRE

7oz large, hand-dived scallops, cleaned
pinch of salt
pinch of ground white pepper

For the stir-fry
2 tablespoons groundnut oil
1-inch piece of ginger, peeled and grated
3 tablespoons Shaohsing rice wine or dry sherry
3½oz fresh samphire, washed and drained
1 tablespoon tamari or low-sodium light soy sauce
1 tablespoon Chinkiang black rice vinegar or balsamic vinegar
2 tablespoons toasted sesame oil

Anything "drunken" is sure to be a winner and this one certainly is! It's a rich and sumptuous dish and the perfect marriage really. Salty samphire gives a pop of savory, while the scallops add a delicious winey sweetness when wokked with the Shaohsing rice wine. In fact, it's the perfect celebratory dish for a Chinese New Year Party. Scallops in Chinese culture symbolise "coins".

Serves 2 kcal 320 carbs 6.4g protein 19g fat 23g

Season the scallops with the salt and white pepper.

Heat a wok over high heat until smoking, add the groundnut oil, and give it a swirl. Add the ginger and quickly stir-fry for a few seconds. Add the seasoned scallops, and cook for 15 seconds, searing them at the edges, then tossing them in the wok. Add the rice wine or dry sherry (if using gas, you can try to catch the flame by tilting the wok near the flames, but be careful when doing this).

Add the samphire to the wok, and stir-fry for 1½ minutes, then season with the tamari or light soy sauce, vinegar, and sesame oil. Cook for another minute until all the scallops have turned opaque and are cooked through, and the samphire has turned a translucent green, but still has a bite. Transfer to a serving dish, and serve with brown or jasmine rice.

5 mins

5 mins

GF DF

TIGER SHRIMPS WITH SWEET AND SOUR RED ONION STIR-FRY

1 tablespoon canola oil

2 red onions, sliced into half-moons

1 tablespoon Shaohsing rice wine or dry sherry

1 teaspoon soft brown sugar

1 tablespoon Chinkiang black rice vinegar or balsamic vinegar

1 green jalapeño chile, seeded and finely chopped

5½oz large cooked and peeled tiger shrimp

1 tablespoon tamari or low-sodium light soy sauce

toasted sesame seeds, for sprinkling

Sweet and sour onions make a delicious base for juicy tiger shrimp in this recipe. Such a quick and easy stir-fry, it's quicker to wok-up this dish than fold your laundry!

Serves 2 kcal 200 carbs 15.4g protein 15g fat 9g

Heat a wok over high heat until smoking, add the canola oil, and give it a swirl. Add the onions, and stir-fry for 2 minutes until they start to turn golden brown at the edges. Then add the rice wine or dry sherry, the brown sugar and vinegar, and toss for 1 minute. Add the green chile pieces, and cook for 30 seconds. Finally, add the cooked tiger shrimp, and toss all the ingredients together. Season with the tamari or light soy sauce, take it off the heat, and add a small sprinkle of toasted sesame seeds. Serve immediately with steamed jasmine rice or brown rice.

BOOZY DRUNKEN SHRIMP

5 mins

5 mins

GF DF

1 tablespoon canola oil

1-inch piece of ginger, peeled and sliced into matchsticks

14oz large raw unshelled freshwater shrimp, or baby shrimp, deveined

3–4 tablespoons Shaohsing rice wine or vodka

1–2 tablespoons tamari or low-sodium light soy sauce

2 pinches of ground white pepper

My grandmother always cooked fresh river shrimp in a variety of ways—sometimes just stir-fried with garlic, ginger, chile, and salt, other times with light soy sauce and scallions. She particularly loved cooking with rice wine—a staple in the Chinese pantry. This recipe is my simple creation inspired by her—the ginger adds warmth and aroma, while the rice wine adds a bitter sweetness that complements the natural sweetness of the shrimp.

Serves 2 kcal 220 carbs 2.8g protein 35.8g fat 7g

Heat a wok over high heat until smoking, add the canola oil, and give the oil a swirl. Add the ginger, and toss quickly in the hot oil for a few seconds. Then add the shrimp, and stir-fry for 2 minutes. Add the rice wine or vodka, and cook for 1 minute. The shrimp are cooked when they have all turned a pinky-orange color. Season with the tamari or light soy sauce and white pepper. Serve immediately with stir-fried vegetables and jasmine rice.

5 mins

5-6 mins

GF DF

HADDOCK, GINGER, AND BABY BOK CHOY SOUP

9oz haddock loin, cut into
⅜-inch slices
1-inch piece of ginger, peeled,
and cut into matchsticks
1 tablespoon Shaohsing rice wine
or dry sherry
3 fresh shiitake mushrooms,
rinsed, patted dry and sliced
4 baby bok choy, sliced in half
down the middle
1 tablespoon vegetable bouillon
powder
dash of toasted sesame oil
pinch of sea salt
pinch of ground white pepper
small handful of cilantro

This is a simple, quick, and nourishing supper. It pays to buy fish from sustainable sources. I find fish from Norway and Iceland particularly delicious—not surprising given their clean, clear waters. You will love the delicate flavors of this soup, which is perfect for someone recovering from illness—it's soothing, light, and full of goodness.

Serves 2 kcal 150 carbs 5g protein 25g fat 3g

Rinse the fish in cold running water. Pour 3½ cups water into a wok, and bring to a boil. Add the fish, and all the ingredients up to and including the bouillon powder. Turn the heat to medium and cook for 5 minutes. Season with the sesame oil, salt, and white pepper, then stir in the cilantro. Transfer to serving bowls and serve immediately.

CRABMEAT SWEETCORN SOUP

2 ripe tomatoes, each sliced into 6 wedges

2 fresh ears of corn, kernels sliced off

1 tablespoon vegetable bouillon powder

9oz fresh white crabmeat, cooked and picked over, ready to eat (or use canned)

2 tablespoons tamari or low-sodium light soy sauce

generous pinch of ground white pepper

1 tablespoon cornstarch, blended with 2 tablespoons cold water

2 large eggs, beaten

large dash of toasted sesame oil

For the garnish

1 scallion, sliced on the diagonal

sprinkle of toasted sesame seeds (optional)

This is a staple soup I reach for time and time again. Perfect as a delicious light supper, it's very versatile and you can also make it more luxurious by adding crayfish tails, shrimp, or even wok-fried scallops or lobster tails.

If you are vegan, substitute the crabmeat for smoked tofu cubes and oyster mushroom pieces, and then follow the rest of the recipe; it will be just as delicious!

Serves 2 kcal 452 carbs 31.1g protein 39.7g fat 19.4g

Pour 1 quart water into a wok and bring to a simmering boil. Add the tomatoes and corn, and cook for 3 minutes to break them down. Keeping the heat on a simmering boil, add the bouillon powder and stir well.

Add the crabmeat, light soy sauce, and white pepper to the soup and stir well. Bring the mixture up to a rolling boil, and stir in the blended cornstarch. Using a fork, create a whirlpool in the stock and stir in the beaten eggs, creating a web-like pattern. Season with the sesame oil, then pour into two bowls.

Garnish with the scallion and sesame seeds, if you like, and serve immediately with some chunky French bread or gluten-free bread.

SMOKED SALMON AND EGG FRIED RICE

1 tablespoon canola oil, plus 1
   teaspoon
2 large scallions, finely sliced
3 eggs, lightly beaten
12oz cooked and cooled jasmine
   rice
3½ oz whiskey oak-smoked
   Scottish salmon, torn into
   large strips
1–2 tablespoons tamari or low-
   sodium light soy sauce
large pinch of freshly ground
   black pepper
½ teaspoon toasted sesame oil
1 teaspoon sriracha chili sauce
   (optional)

I always cook more rice so I have some left over for this easy
and super delicious dish. Just fire up the wok, add oil, fry
some scallions, pour in a few beaten eggs, stir to scramble,
then add the rice and toss together well, adding in chunky
slices of your favorite smoked salmon, then season with soy
sauce, black pepper, and a small dash of toasted sesame oil
for nuttiness and you're done! For a zingy, fiery note, a small
drizzle of sriracha or your favorite chili oil will wrap the whole
dish up nicely.

For a vegan version, swap the smoked salmon for smoked
tofu strips and sliced fresh shiitake mushrooms, it will be
just as delish!

Serves 2 kcal 413 carbs 42.6g protein 25g fat 17g

Heat a wok over high heat until smoking, add the 1 tablespoon of
canola oil, and give the oil a swirl. Add the scallions, and stir-fry
for a few seconds, then add the beaten eggs, and stir-fry for
1 minute to scramble into small moist pieces. Push the eggs to
one side.

Add the 1 teaspoon of canola oil and the jasmine rice to the wok
and fry together for 1 minute, then add the smoked salmon, and
toss until all the ingredients are thoroughly combined.

Season with the tamari or light soy sauce, black pepper, and
sesame oil, and toss together well. Serve immediately with some
sriracha chili sauce, if you like.

CHICKEN

& DUCK

10 mins

5 mins

GF DF

BLACK PEPPER DUCK AND KALE WOKKED RICE

For the duck

7oz duck breasts, skinned and finely diced

¼ teaspoon cracked black pepper

1 teaspoon Shaohsing rice wine or dry sherry

1 teaspoon dark soy sauce

5 tablespoons canola oil

1 teaspoon cornstarch

For the fried rice

3½oz kale, finely chopped

1 garlic clove, minced

1 tablespoon peeled and grated ginger

1 red bell pepper, deseeded and diced

1½ cups cooked brown rice (scant ½ cup uncooked)

2oz green beans, finely chopped

2 tablespoons tamari or low-sodium light soy sauce

1 teaspoon toasted sesame oil

pinch of ground black pepper

juice of 1 lemon, to serve

Inspired by my love of Macanese black pepper roast duck, which is served with Cantonese *gai lan* (Chinese broccoli) and rice, I wanted to have all the flavors of the duck and greens in the rice and so here it is—a simple, quick, and delicious duck wokked rice.

Serves 2 kcal 526 carbs 61.3g protein 29.9g fat 19.7g

Season the duck with the cracked black pepper, rice wine or dry sherry, and dark soy sauce. Sprinkle over the cornflour and set aside.

Heat a wok over high heat until smoking, add the canola oil, and give it a swirl. Add the duck pieces, and stir-fry for 2–3 minutes until well-done and slightly crisp. Pour the duck and oil into a heatproof colander set over a heatproof bowl, and drain the duck well, reserving the oil.

Reheat the wok, and add 1 tablespoon of the drained oil. Add the kale, garlic, and ginger, and stir-fry for 4–5 seconds. Add the red bell pepper and stir-fry for 30 seconds.

Add the duck, rice, green beans, tamari or light soy sauce, sesame oil, and black pepper, and stir-fry for 10–15 seconds until the rice and vegetables are mixed well with the soy sauce, and everything is heated through. Dress the rice with a squeeze of fresh lemon juice, and serve immediately.

15 mins

18 mins

GF DF

GENERAL TSO'S CHICKEN WINGS

sunflower oil, for deep-frying
18oz chicken wings, separated at
    the joints
pinch of salt
pinch of ground white pepper
2 garlic cloves, smashed
4 dried red chiles, roughly
    chopped

For the sauce
1¼ cups chicken stock
scant ½ cup tomato ketchup
3 tablespoons yellow bean paste
    or miso paste
3 tablespoons cornstarch
2 tablespoons sriracha chili
    sauce
1 tablespoon Shaohsing rice wine
    or dry sherry
2 tablespoons runny honey
2 tablespoons tamari or low-
    sodium light soy sauce
1½ tablespoons soft brown sugar
1 teaspoon dark soy sauce

For the garnish
toasted white sesame seeds
scallions, sliced into rounds

Sticky, sweet, and spicy, this is an easy-to-make, finger lickin' good crowd pleaser.

If you are vegan, you can use fried tofu and vegetable stock—just make the sauce, toss in the tofu, wok-fry, then grill until the tofu is sticky. Such a versatile dish. Enjoy!

Serves 4 kcal 701 carbs 81.7g protein 39.9g fat 26.3g

Heat a large wok or deep-fryer over high heat, then fill to a third of its depth with sunflower oil. Heat the oil to 350°F, or until a bread cube dropped in the oil turns golden brown in 15 seconds, and floats to the surface.

Season the chicken wings with the salt and white pepper, and deep-fry for 12–15 minutes until golden brown and cooked through. Drain on paper towels.

For the sauce, pour all the ingredients into a large jug, and whisk to combine.

Heat a wok over high heat until smoking, add 2–3 tablespoons of sunflower oil, and give it a swirl. Add the garlic and dried chiles, and toss for a few seconds, then add the sauce, and cook until slightly reduced and the consistency of gravy. Reserve a cupful of sauce, enough to fill a dipping bowl, then toss in the chicken wings.

Preheat the broiler to high. Place the wings on a baking sheet, and broil for about 2 minutes, until the sauce is bubbling. Remove, transfer to a large serving plate, and garnish with toasted sesame seeds and sliced scallions. Serve with the reserved sauce to dip.

30 mins

5 mins

DF

CHICKEN AND CHINESE CELERY BOILED WONTONS IN A SICHUAN-CHINKIANG VINEGAR DRESSING

For the filling
1 lb ground chicken
3 oz dried shiitake mushrooms
3 tablespoons finely chopped Chinese celery with leaves
1 tablespoon peeled and finely grated ginger
1 tablespoon tamari or low-sodium light soy sauce
1 tablespoon cornstarch
1 tablespoon Shaohsing rice wine or dry sherry
1 tablespoon chicken bouillon powder
1 teaspoon toasted sesame oil
1 teaspoon salt
1 egg white
1/2 teaspoon ground white pepper

For the wontons
cornstarch, for dusting
6¼ x 3-inch wonton wrappers

For the vinegar sauce
2 tablespoons tamari or low-sodium light soy sauce
2 tablespoons chili oil
1 tablespoon Chinkiang black rice or balsamic vinegar
1/2 teaspoon Sichuan peppercorns, crushed
1 teaspoon toasted sesame oil

For the garnish
chopped cucumber
cilantro leaves

This is one of those healthy Chinese dishes that is low in calories, yet feels so satisfying and comforting. The chicken is delicate, and the aniseed notes of the celery work so well with the seasoning of white pepper. The wontons are served with a Sichuan pepper and Chinkiang black rice vinegar—fusing Chinese west and Chinese east. I like to make a whole large batch of these, and then boil them from frozen for a quick, easy dinner. For a more substantial dinner, serve with some noodles and plenty of chili oil.

Makes 16 kcal 101 carbs 11.7g protein 8.5g fat 2.6g*

For the filling, soak the shiitake mushrooms in hot water for 15 minutes, then drain, discard the stalks, and finely chop. In a bowl, combine them with the chicken, celery, ginger, tamari or light soy sauce, cornstarch, rice wine or dry sherry, the chicken bouillon powder, sesame oil, salt, egg white, and white pepper. Mix well and set aside.

For the wontons, line a baking sheet with parchment paper, and dust lightly with cornstarch. Take one wonton wrapper and place 1 teaspoon of the filling in the center. Gather up the sides, and mold around the filling, making a ball shape, and twisting the top to secure. Repeat with the remaining wrappers and filling, lining them up on the prepared baking sheet.

Drop the wontons into boiling water in a wok and cook until they float to the surface, about 3–5 minutes.

Combine all the ingredients for the vinegar sauce in a bowl, and stir.

To serve, divide the wontons between two plates. Surround with the chopped cucumber, drizzle with the vinegar sauce and top with the cilantro. Serve immediately.

*per wonton

15 mins

60 mins

GF

MACANESE-STYLE CHICKEN CURRY

2 tablespoons vegetable oil

2lb mixed chicken thighs and drumsticks, skinned, bone in, each piece halved through the bone (ask your butcher to prepare this for you)

1lb new potatoes, skin on

1¾ cups glutinous rice

3½oz broccolini or Chinese *gai lan* broccoli, cut on the diagonal into 2-inch pieces

salt and ground white pepper, to taste

For the curry

2 tablespoons unsalted butter

1 tablespoon vegetable oil

3 garlic cloves, minced

3 small shallots, diced

2 onions, diced

2 tablespoons Madras curry powder

2oz dried coconut

5oz eggplants, roll cut, then sliced into 2-inch finger slices

9fl oz canned coconut milk

generous 2 cups chicken stock

3 tablespoons tamarind paste

This is essentially a rich coconut chicken curry cooked low and slow in the wok, so that the meat melts and becomes very tender. Inspired by the rich fusion of cultures in Macau—Portuguese, African, Chinese, and Indian—and using tamarind paste borrowed from Africa. It's a great dish for entertaining because you can cook it in advance. Chopping the chicken through the bone adds flavor, but rinse the pieces in cold water afterward to remove any splintered bits of bone, or ask your butcher to do it.

Serves 6 kcal 726 carbs 66.6g protein 37.0g fat 37.3g

Heat a wok over high heat until smoking, add the vegetable oil, and give it a swirl. Add the chicken and brown for 3–4 minutes. Remove the chicken from the wok, set aside, and reheat the wok to medium.

To make the curry, add the butter and vegetable oil to the wok, and fry the garlic, shallots, onions, and curry powder for 2 minutes until the onions are translucent. Add the chicken, dried coconut, and eggplant slices and stir-fry for 2–3 minutes. Add the coconut milk, chicken stock, and tamarind paste, and bring to a simmer, then simmer on medium heat for 35–40 minutes until the chicken is cooked through, and falling off the bone.

Meanwhile, cook the potatoes in a pan of boiling salted water for 15 minutes, then drain, and set aside.

While the curry is simmering, wash the rice in a strainer until the water runs clear. Place in a medium pot, and cover with 2½ cups water. Bring to a boil, reduce the heat to low, cover the pan, and simmer for 15–20 minutes until all the water has been absorbed. Fluff up the grains, cover, and keep it warm on the stove top.

Add the cooked potatoes to the curry and cook for 10 minutes. Then stir in the broccolini and cook for two minutes. Season to taste with salt and white pepper, remove from the heat, and serve immediately with the rice.

Prep time: 1 hour marinade
Oven time: 40 mins for the duck

2 x 14oz duck legs

For the marinade
2 garlic cloves, minced
2 tablespoons peeled and grated
    ginger
1 tablespoon Shaohsing rice wine
    or dry sherry
1 teaspoon Chinese five-spice
    powder
2 tablespoons runny honey
2 tablespoons hoisin sauce
1 tablespoon dark soy sauce
pinch of sea salt

For the wontons
peanut oil, for deep-frying
about 20—30 wonton wrappers
pinch of salt
pinch of ground white pepper
finely chopped chives

To serve
2—3 tablespoons hoisin sauce
sliced strawberries

For the dressing (optional)
1 tablespoon plum sauce
1 tablespoon hoisin sauce
2 tablespoons olive oil
2 tablespoons lime juice
pinch of superfine sugar
1 teaspoon tamari or low-sodium
    light soy sauce

HOISIN DUCK AND STRAWBERRY WOK-FRIED CRISPY WONTON 'TACOS'

I was messing around with wonton wrappers, and came up with the idea for turning them into little crispy "tacos". Great for gatherings, they're easy to make, and can be cooked in advance, and assembled when the party gets started. The fresh strawberry slices add a lovely pop of sweetness. Although you need to allow time for prep, they are assembled very quickly.

Serves 4 kcal 477 carbs 46.7g protein 17.2g fat 25g

Place the duck legs in a ziplock bag. Add all the marinade ingredients, turn to coat the legs, and marinate in the fridge for at least 1 hour. If using, whisk all the ingredients for the dressing in a bowl and set aside.

Preheat the oven to 350°F. Place the duck legs (and the marinade) round-side up on a roasting pan lined with foil, and roast for 40 minutes, then increase the heat to 425°F, and roast for another 10 minutes, until well-done. Remove from the oven, transfer to a plate, and carefully pour the cooking juices into a heatproof pitcher. Leave the duck to rest, then shred the meat when cool to the touch (discarding the bones). Keep covered in a warm oven until ready to serve. Mix the cooking juices with the hoisin sauce (to serve), and set aside.

Heat a wok over medium-high heat and fill to a third of its depth with peanut oil. Heat the oil to 300°F, or until a bread cube dropped in the oil turns golden brown in 15 seconds, and floats to the surface. Deep-fry the wontons in batches for 40 seconds until golden and crispy. Turn out onto paper towels, then sprinkle with salt, white pepper, and chives and toss to coat.

To serve, top each wonton with some shredded duck, drizzle over the hoisin mixture, and garnish with the sliced strawberries and more chives.

Ching's Tip
Turn this dish into a salad by serving on some watercress – spread the duck on the leaves, top with the hoisin mixture and broken-up pieces of wontons and garnish with strawberries.

SWEET SPICY CHICKEN WITH CRISPY GREEN PEPPERS

1lb chicken thighs, boned and skinned, sliced into ¼-inch strips
1 tablespoon chili bean paste
2 tablespoons cornstarch
canola oil, for deep-frying
pinch of sea salt
3 long dried chiles
1 large green bell pepper, seeded, and sliced into ⅜-inch strips
1 large white onion, cut into half-moon slices
1 tablespoon tamari or low-sodium light soy sauce
3 tablespoons sweet chili sauce
juice of ½ medium orange
1/2 teaspoon dark soy sauce
1 scallion, sliced lengthways, to garnish

This is one of those quick and delicious easy winner dinners. Seasoning the chicken with chili bean paste—a fiery Sichuan paste of soybeans and chile that is rich in umami and heat in equal measure—ensures it has bags of flavor. Then coating it with a light dusting of cornstarch locks in the flavor and the moisture. Jasmine rice is the perfect accompaniment to soak up the delish flavors of the sauce.

For a vegan version, use sliced king trumpet mushrooms, or sliced fresh shiitake mushrooms, and just wok-fry with the crispy green peppers.

Serves 2 kcal 648 carbs 48g protein 50g fat 30.8g

Place the chicken strips in a large bowl and season with the chili bean paste. Mix well, then the add cornstarch and toss until the chicken has absorbed it.

Heat a wok over high heat, and fill to a third of its depth with canola oil. Heat the oil to 350°F, or until a bread cube dropped in the oil turns golden brown in 15 seconds and floats to the surface. Frying in batches, lower the chicken into the oil, and cook until golden brown, about 5 minutes, then drain on paper towels. Drain the oil through a heatproof colander set over a heatproof bowl.

Reheat the wok over high heat, and add 1 teaspoon of the oil, and a pinch of sea salt, add the onion and dried chiles and wok-fry for a few seconds to release their aroma. Add the green bell pepper, and toss-cook them for 30 seconds to sear and crisp at the edges. Then add the tamari or light soy sauce, chili sauce, orange juice and dark soy sauce and bring to a bubble. Add the chicken and toss together with the peppers to coat well, then serve immediately with jasmine rice and top with the scallion.

GF DF

CHING'S CHICKEN CHAU CHAU PARIDA

1 tablespoon canola oil

3 garlic cloves, minced

1 knob of ginger, peeled and
finely chopped

2 scallions, sliced into ⅜-inch
rounds

2 pinches of sea salt

1 teaspoon ground turmeric

18oz chicken thighs, skinned,
boned, and sliced into 1-inch
chunks

¼ cup Shaohsing rice wine or
dry sherry

1 tablespoon tamari or low-
sodium light soy sauce

1 tablespoon Chinkiang black
rice vinegar or balsamic
vinegar

3 grinds of cracked black pepper

7oz broccolini stems, par-boiled
for 1 minute

This recipe is inspired by the Macanese "Chau Chau Parida", a stir-fried dish usually eaten by Chinese mothers to replace the "yang" energy after giving birth. This is a restorative dish, and delicious with some sweet broccolini added in. The gingery, warm, savory, and winey notes work well with plain jasmine rice.

Serves 2 kcal 536 carbs 9.5g protein 57.3g fat 30.7g

Heat a wok over high heat until smoking, add the canola oil, and give the oil a swirl. Add the garlic, ginger, scallions, sea salt, and turmeric, and cook for 10 seconds to release their aroma.

Add the chicken pieces, and sear on one side for 30 seconds, then toss and cook for 2–3 minutes until browned all over. Before the chicken is completely cooked, add the rice wine or dry sherry. Cook for 1 minute to reduce the wine, then add the tamari or light soy sauce, vinegar, and season with the black pepper. Toss in the par-boiled broccolini. Remove from the heat, and serve with jasmine rice.

OYSTER SAUCE CHICKEN WITH NAPA CABBAGE

10½oz chicken thighs, boned, skinned, and sliced into ⅜-inch strips

2 scallions, sliced on the diagonal, to garnish

For the marinade
pinch of salt
pinch of ground white pepper
1 tablespoon oyster sauce
1 tablespoon cornstarch

For the stir-fry
2 tablespoons canola oil
1 garlic clove, minced
1-inch piece of ginger, peeled and grated
1 red chile, seeded and finely chopped
1 tablespoon Shaohsing rice wine or dry sherry
5oz Napa cabbage, sliced into 2-inch chunks

For the sauce
scant ⅕ cup hot vegetable stock
2 tablespoons tamari or low-sodium light soy sauce
1 teaspoon toasted sesame oil

This is a Beijing-meets-Canton-style home-wokked dish. Whenever I eat Napa cabbage, which is also called Chinese leaf, it reminds me of the Shandong province and their obsession with leafy cabbage vegetables—a symbol of peasant food. Oyster sauce was created in Guangdong, and is a secret umami savory weapon I cannot live without in my pantry. The oyster sauce makes the chicken super addictive, and works so well with the Napa cabbage, which lends a delicious sweet bite once softened. The wok juices are perfect drizzled over jasmine rice.

If you're vegan, you can use firm tofu instead of the chicken, and use vegetarian oyster sauce – it would be equally delish.

Serves 2 kcal 437 carbs 18.8g protein 41.7g fat 36g

Put the chicken and all the ingredients for the marinade in a bowl, and turn to coat.

Heat a wok over high heat until smoking, then add 1 tablespoon of the canola oil and give it a swirl. Add the garlic, ginger, and chile, and stir-fry for a few seconds, then add the chicken. Wok-fry the chicken for 2 minutes until it starts to caramelize, and turn opaque. Add the rice wine or dry sherry, and deglaze the wok. Cook for another 2 minutes, until the chicken is cooked through. Spoon out onto a plate.

Reheat the wok over high heat until smoking, then add the remaining canola oil, and give it a swirl. Add the Napa cabbage, and stir-fry for 1 minute, then add about 2 tablespoons cold water to help create some steam to cook the leaves. Pour in all the sauce ingredients, and bring to a boil. Once the cabbage has wilted, spoon out onto serving plates, top with the chicken pieces, and garnish with the scallions. Serve with jasmine rice.

10 mins

25 mins

DF

STEAMED SICHUAN HOT AND SOUR CHICKEN

4 boneless, skinless chicken
thighs
2 tablespoons Shaohsing rice
wine or dry sherry
pinch of sea salt
pinch of ground white pepper
1 tablespoon cornstarch
1-inch piece of ginger, peeled,
and sliced into matchsticks
2 large scallions, sliced
lengthwise
7oz broccolini, sliced on an angle

For the dressing
2 tablespoons tamari or low-
sodium light soy sauce
1 teaspoon toasted sesame oil
2 garlic cloves, minced
1-inch piece of ginger, peeled,
and finely grated
1 red chile, seeded and finely
chopped
1 tablespoon Sichuan mustard
pickle in chili oil, finely
chopped
3 tablespoons canola oil
1 teaspoon dark soy sauce
2 tablespoons rice vinegar
pinch of soft brown sugar

This is a super healthy and easy recipe. The dressing combines raw garlic and ginger, and is pungent, bold, and full of flavor —if you can't get the Sichuan mustard pickle just do without, though if you can it's worth every bite.

Serves 2 kcal 559 carbs 18.8g protein 41.7g fat 36g

Place the chicken in a heatproof bowl (that can fit inside a steamer), and drizzle with the rice wine or dry sherry. Season the chicken with the salt, white pepper, and cornstarch, then place the ginger matchsticks on top of the chicken, and drape half the scallion slices over.

Place the bowl in a bamboo steamer, cover with a lid, and steam over a wok of simmering water (making sure the water does not touch the base of the steamer) for 15–20 minutes (depending on the size of the thighs), or until the chicken is cooked through. Check the water level during cooking, and top up with boiling water if necessary.

Place all the dressing ingredients in a bowl, and stir to combine.

In a separate pan, bring 3 cups water to a boil, add the broccolini, and blanch for 2 minutes. Remove and drain, then transfer to a serving plate and drizzle with 1 tablespoon of the dressing.

Remove the chicken from the steamer. Pour any cooking juices into the dressing and mix. Transfer the chicken to a cutting board, and chop into long, rectangular chunks. Place over the broccolini, and spoon over the remaining dressing. Garnish with the remaining scallion slices, and serve immediately.

10 mins

8 mins

GF DF

THAI-INSPIRED CHICKEN COCONUT BROTH

14oz boneless, skinless chicken thighs, sliced into 1-inch chunks
pinch of sea salt
pinch of ground white pepper
1 teaspoon cornstarch
1 tablespoon canola oil
2 stalks of lemongrass, sliced into 1-inch pieces
2 cups hot vegetable stock
½ cup coconut milk
1 kaffir lime leaf, whole
2 ripe tomatoes, quartered, skin on
7oz oyster mushrooms
2 tablespoons fish sauce
juice of 1 lime
½ teaspoon superfine sugar
cilantro, to garnish

This is a healthy, light, coconut chicken broth dinner. Sometimes I love a soup for dinner, especially if I've had a heavy day of eating. For me, the key to keeping the chicken succulent and moist, is to wok-fry and seal it first. Then add all the rest of the ingredients. It's quick, and makes a delicious light supper.

Vegans can substitute the chicken with extra meaty oyster mushrooms.

Serves 2 kcal 520 carbs 13.2g protein 46.6g fat 34.7g

Put the chicken in a bowl and season with the salt, white pepper, and cornstarch.

Heat a wok over high heat until smoking, add the canola oil, and give it a swirl. Add the lemongrass, and toss for a few seconds to release its aroma. Add the chicken, and sear for a few seconds, then cook, tossing, for 2–3 minutes until almost cooked through. Add the hot vegetable stock, coconut milk, lime leaf, tomatoes, and mushrooms. Season with the fish sauce, lime juice, and superfine sugar and bring to a boil. Then turn the heat down to medium, and simmer for another 2 minutes. Remove from the heat, garnish with cilantro, and serve.

20 mins

5-6 mins

GF DF

CHICKEN, SHRIMP AND MUSHROOM CONGEE

1 tablespoon canola oil

1 tablespoon peeled and finely grated ginger

2 boneless, skinless chicken thighs, finely diced

1 tablespoon Shaohsing rice wine, dry sherry, or vegetable stock

3½oz dried Chinese shrimp, soaked in hot water for 15 minutes, drained, and finely chopped

4 dried Chinese mushrooms, soaked in hot water for 20 minutes, drained, stalks discarded, and diced

1 tablespoon tamari or low-sodium light soy sauce

1 tablespoon oyster sauce

pinch of sea salt

pinch of ground white pepper

1 tablespoon toasted sesame oil

1 recipe quantity Classic Plain Congee "Zhou" (see page 52)

handful of baby spinach leaves, rolled and sliced

handful of finely chopped cilantro

1 scallion, finely chopped

This surf 'n' turf combination of chicken and seafood is so Asia. I love pork congee, but chicken works just as well, too. The trick is to use chicken thighs off the bone, diced very finely. Use dried shrimp as well, as they are full of flavor. This is a flavorful and delicious dish, and my own proud invention. I hope you enjoy it.

Serves 6 kcal 310 carbs 44g protein 19.9g fat 7.4g

Heat a wok over high heat until smoking, add the canola oil, and give the oil a swirl. Add the ginger and chicken, and stir-fry quickly for 3 minutes until the chicken is almost cooked. Add the rice wine, dry sherry or vegetable stock, the Chinese shrimp, and mushrooms, and stir-fry until fragrant and the chicken is cooked through.

Season with the tamari or light soy sauce, oyster sauce, salt, white pepper and sesame oil. Add the chicken mixture to the congee, and stir well. Check the seasoning and season more to your taste if necessary. Stir the spinach, chopped cilantro, and scallion through, and serve immediately.

2 mins

3-4 mins

GF DF

CHICKEN WITH GINGER CHOY SUM AND GOJI BERRIES

For the chicken

9oz boneless chicken thighs, skinned, and sliced into 1-inch chunks

pinch of dried red pepper flakes

½ teaspoon Chinese five-spice powder

pinch of sea salt

pinch of ground white pepper

1 tablespoon cornstarch

1 tablespoon canola oil

2 tablespoons Shaohsing rice wine or dry sherry

1 tablespoon tamari or low-sodium light soy sauce

1 teaspoon toasted sesame oil

small handful of dried goji berries, soaked in warm water for 5 minutes, drained

For the stir-fry

1 tablespoon canola oil

pinch of sea salt

1-inch piece of ginger, peeled and grated

14oz Chinese *choy sum* (or broccolini or bok choy), washed and sliced into 2-inch pieces

3 tablespoons hot vegetable stock

Before she turned veggie, my mother used to make steamed Shaohsing rice wine chicken with goji berries and ginger. I have turned it into a stir-fry because I love the wok-seared taste of the chicken when it cooks in the wok together with the *choy sum* (though bok choy would be delicious too), and the bitter sweetness of the goji berries. A quick, simple, healthy recipe that is energizing, and full of goodness.

You can make this one vegan by substituting meaty oyster mushrooms for the chicken.

Serves 2 kcal 437 carbs 26.9g protein 36.9g fat 21.1g

Season the chicken with the dried red pepper flakes, Chinese five-spice powder, salt, and white pepper, and dust with the cornstarch. Set aside.

For the stir-fry, heat a wok over high heat until smoking, then add 1 tablespoon canola oil, and a pinch of salt. Give it a swirl. Add the ginger, and stir-fry for a few seconds to release its aroma. Add the Chinese *choy sum* (or broccoli or bok choy), and stir-fry for 1 minute, tossing it in the wok. Add the hot stock around the edges, then transfer to a warm serving plate.

Finish the chicken. Reheat the wok until smoking, add 1 tablespoon canola oil, and give the oil a swirl. Add the chicken pieces, and sear for 30 seconds, then toss to turn and cook the chicken for 2 minutes over high heat. Add the rice wine or dry sherry and cook, tossing and stirring, for another 2 minutes until the chicken is cooked through. Season with the tamari or light soy sauce and sesame oil. Stir in the goji berries, and give it one last toss. Spoon out on top of the *choy sum* and serve immediately. Perfect with jasmine rice.

10 mins

15 mins

DF

CHILE CHICKEN AND CHINESE BROCCOLI NOODLE SOUP

5¼ oz dried buckwheat or wheat flour noodles

1 teaspoon toasted sesame oil

1 tablespoon canola oil

few pinches of cracked sea salt

2 small garlic cloves, roughly chopped

1-inch piece of ginger, peeled and finely grated

1 large red cayenne chile pepper, seeded and sliced

2 boneless skinless chicken breasts, sliced thinly on the diagonal

1 tablespoon Shaohsing rice wine or dry sherry

1 tablespoon chili bean paste

1 tablespoon vegetable bouillon powder

2 tablespoons Chinkiang black rice vinegar or balsamic vinegar

1 tablespoon tamari or low-sodium light soy sauce

pinch of soft brown sugar

1 teaspoon toasted sesame oil

5oz *gai lan* (Chinese broccoli), broccolini, or bok choy, sliced on the diagonal into 1-inch pieces

1 scallion, sliced on a deep angle, to garnish

The ginger and chiles give this a perfect warming heat, and the broccoli (whether you choose a Chinese or Western variety) is full of antioxidants. I prefer thin, rather than thick noodles, but it's up to you.

You can make this dish vegan by substituting sliced shiitake mushrooms and smoked tofu for the chicken.

Serves 2 kcal 568 carbs 64.7g protein 50.2g fat 11.2g

Cook the noodles according to the package instructions, then drain, and dress with the toasted sesame oil.

Heat a wok over high heat until smoking, add the canola oil, and give the oil a swirl. Add the sea salt to dissolve in the oil. Add the garlic, ginger, and chile, and stir-fry for a few seconds to release their aroma. Add the chicken slices, and sear for 1 minute, then toss and stir-fry for 2–3 minutes. Season with the rice wine or dry sherry, then add 5 cups boiling water, the chili bean paste, bouillon powder, vinegar, tamari or light soy sauce, brown sugar, and sesame oil. Stir well, and bring the broth to a simmer. Drop in the broccoli or bok choy, and cook for 1 minute.

Divide the noodles between two bowls, pour in the broth, garnish with the scallion, and serve immediately.

20 mins

5–6 mins

GF DF

FIVE-SPICE SAUCY CHICKEN STIR-FRY

10oz boneless, skinless chicken thighs, sliced ³/₈-inch thick
pinch of cracked sea salt
pinch of cracked black pepper
1 teaspoon Chinese five-spice powder
1 tablespoon cornstarch
1 tablespoon canola oil
2 garlic cloves, minced
1-inch piece of ginger, peeled and grated
1 fat jalapeño chile, seeded and finely chopped
3¹/₂oz Chantenay carrots or baby carrots
1 tablespoon tamari or low-sodium light soy sauce
5 baby leeks, cut on an angle into ³/₈-inch slices
8 Savoy cabbage leaves, shredded

For the sauce
²/₃ cup cold vegetable stock or chicken stock
2 tablespoons tamari or low-sodium light soy sauce
1 teaspoon dark soy sauce
1 tablespoon cornstarch

This is my take on bringing the flavors of a Sunday roast right into a wok fry! Call me crazy, but this dish is super delicious, and the sauce delivers on that intoxicating "chickeny gravy" flavor—as they say, it's all gravy, baby, and this one happens to be laced with delicious five-spice.

You can vegan-fy this recipe by using a combination of meaty oyster mushrooms and sliced shiitake mushrooms instead of the chicken.

Serves 2 kcal 545 carbs 34.7g protein 34.2g fat 31.5g

Combine all the ingredients for the sauce in a small jug and mix well.

Put the chicken in a bowl, then season with the salt, black pepper, five-spice powder and cornstarch and toss together. Set aside.

Heat a wok over high heat until smoking, add the canola oil, and give it a swirl. Add the garlic, ginger, and chile, and stir for a few seconds to release their aroma. Then add the carrots, and stir-fry for just over 1 minute. Add the chicken slices, and sear for a few seconds, then toss together for 3–4 minutes. Season with the tamari or light soy sauce, then add the leeks and cabbage, and stir-fry together for 1 minute.

Add the sauce, and bring to a bubble to thicken. Stir and mix well. Transfer to serving plates, and serve with boiled or roast new potatoes and jasmine rice.

GF DF

MALAYSIAN-STYLE FRIED CHICKEN WITH OKRA ON JASMINE RICE

For the spice paste

2 garlic cloves, crushed

1-inch piece of ginger, peeled and grated

½ teaspoon ground cumin

½ teaspoon ground fennel

½ teaspoon ground coriander

½ teaspoon ground cloves

½ teaspoon ground cinnamon

2 green cardamom pods

2 curry leaves

1 teaspoon ground turmeric

1 teaspoon dried red pepper flakes

pinch of salt

For the stir-fry

14oz boneless, skinless chicken thighs, sliced into 1-inch chunks

1 tablespoon canola oil

½ cup coconut milk

3½oz okra, sliced in half on the diagonal

2 tablespoons vegetable stock

pinch of sea salt

pinch of soft brown sugar

juice of 1 lime

This includes one of my pop-in-law's spice mixes that he uses for his famous curry dishes. I've turned it on its head by using it to make a wok-curried, stir-fry supper with chicken and okra. If you're not a fan of okra, then leave it out.

For a vegan version, use meaty oyster mushrooms and tofu instead of the chicken.

Serves 4 kcal 226 carbs 2.1g protein 23.1g fat 16.5g

Using a stick blender or a special spice blender/clean coffee grinder, grind all the ingredients for the spice paste with 3 tablespoons water. Add to the chicken in a bowl, and toss to mix well.

Heat a wok over high heat until smoking, add the canola oil, and swirl it around. Stir-fry the chicken for 5 minutes until cooked through, then add the coconut milk, and cook until the chicken has absorbed it, and the sauce has reduced down. Add the okra and vegetable stock, and toss for 1 minute. Season with the sea salt, brown sugar, and lime juice. Serve with jasmine rice.

TURMERIC CHICKEN PEPPER STIR-FRY

½ teaspoon ground turmeric

½ teaspoon dried red pepper flakes

½ teaspoon ground coriander

2 boneless chicken breasts, skinned and sliced into ⅜-inch strips

1 tablespoon canola oil

1-inch piece of ginger, peeled and grated

1 tablespoon Shaohsing rice wine or dry sherry

2 tablespoons vegetable stock

1 red bell pepper, seeded and cut into julienne strips

1 green bell pepper, seeded and cut into julienne strips

small handful of snow peas

1 tablespoon tamari or low-sodium light soy sauce

juice of 1 lemon

scant ¼ cup salted cashew nuts, crushed in a mortar and pestle or roughly chopped

You can load as much crunchy veg as you wish into this spiced chicken stir-fry. Simple and quick, it packs in protein, veg, and flavor for an easy one wok-dinner!

Serves 2 kcal 375 carbs 15.5g protein 43.8g fat 15.5g

Combine the turmeric, red pepper flakes, ground coriander in a bowl. Add the chicken strips and toss to mix well.

Heat a wok over high heat until smoking, add the canola oil, and give the oil a swirl to coat the sides of the wok. Add the ginger, fry for a few seconds, then add the spiced chicken slices and sear for a few seconds to release their aroma and flavor into the oil. Flip the chicken, and toss for 3–4 minutes so that it colors and caramelizes at the edges. Add the rice wine or dry sherry followed by the stock. Quickly add the red and green pepper strips and snow peas and stir-fry for 1 minute.

Season with the tamari or light soy sauce and the lemon juice. Tip in the cashew nuts, and eat immediately.

PORK, BEEF

& LAMB

10 mins

5 mins

GF DF

WOK-FRIED BEEF IN CHILI SAUCE WITH CILANTRO

1 tablespoon canola oil
1 garlic clove, crushed
7oz beef fillet, sliced into strips
1 tablespoon Shaohsing rice wine
    or dry sherry
3½oz snow peas
8oz canned water chestnuts,
    drained and sliced
chopped cilantro, to garnish

For the sauce
3oz peanuts, crushed until
    smooth, or use smooth peanut
    butter
1 teaspoon toasted Sichuan
    pepper (toasted and ground)
1 teaspoon runny honey
2 tablespoons tamari or low-
    sodium light soy sauce
1 teaspoon chili oil
1 teaspoon toasted sesame oil
1 teaspoon Chinkiang black rice
    vinegar or balsamic vinegar
1 teaspoon chili bean paste or
    your favorite chili sauce
pinch of salt

I love simple, easy, straightforward suppers such as this one. Go wild like Tom Cruise in *Cocktail* when creating the sauce —infuse, shake, juggle, and stir!

This dish is perfect with plain jasmine rice and extra steamed greens on the side. For vegans, substitute smoked tofu slices and sliced fresh shiitake mushrooms for the beef, and golden syrup for the honey.

Serves 2 kcal 498 carbs 18g protein 36.3g fat 31.4g

Combine all the ingredients for the sauce in a small bowl and mix well. Set aside.

Heat a wok over high heat until smoking, add the canola oil, and give the oil a swirl. Add the garlic, and fry for a few seconds, then add the beef strips, and sear for a few seconds on one side, then flip over. Season with the rice wine or dry sherry. Add the snow peas and water chestnuts, and toss for 1 minute. Pour in the sauce, and toss together well until all the ingredients have been coated. Garnish with chopped cilantro and serve.

BEEF AND PEA WONTONS

15–20 mins

5–6 mins

DF

16 wonton wrappers, or pasta or
    ravioli sheets

For the filling
2oz ground beef
2oz frozen peas, defrosted
1 teaspoon peeled and grated
    ginger
1 teaspoon Shaohsing rice wine
    or dry sherry
1 scallion, finely chopped
1 teaspoon vegetable bouillon
    powder
pinch of sea salt
pinch of ground white pepper

To serve
good store-bought or homemade
    gravy of your choice
chiu chow chili oil
crushed peanuts

* per wonton

When I'm in need of comfort, these are my go-to wontons, particularly as they are so easy to make—just wrap and twist, no need for fiddling around with pleats. I use ground beef in these dumplings and peas for texture, and I like to serve them with good old English gravy and a splash of Chinese chili oil. Wok's not to love? A bit of British Chineseness never hurt anyone.

If you're vegan, use textured vegetable protein (TVP) instead of ground beef, and then follow the rest of the recipe.

Makes 16 kcal 41 carbs 6g protein 2.2g fat 0.9g*

Mix together all the ingredients for the filling in a bowl.

Take a teaspoon of the filling and place in the center of a wonton wrapper. Gather the four sides, and pinch and twist to seal. Repeat with the rest of the filling and wonton wrappers.

Steam or boil in a wok for 8 minutes (see tip). Remove and pour over plenty of gravy. Spoon over some *Chiu Chow* Chili Oil, and garnish with crushed peanuts. Serve immediately.

Ching's Tip
Or deep-fry in hot oil at 350°F for 2–3 minutes until the wontons are golden, and the inside is cooked. Drain on paper towel before serving.

15 mins

7 mins

DF

BEEF AND MUSHROOM BEIJING-STYLE WHEAT FLOUR PANCAKES

10oz sirloin steak, cut into ³/₈-inch dice
pinch of salt
pinch of ground white pepper
1 teaspoon Shaohsing rice wine or dry sherry
1 tablespoon oyster sauce
1 tablespoon canola oil
5 dried Chinese mushrooms, soaked in hot water for 15 minutes, drained, stalks discarded, finely diced
1 tablespoon tamari or low-sodium light soy sauce
1 teaspoon toasted sesame oil
2 Chinese garlic chives or scallions, sliced into ¹/₈-inch pieces
10 store-bought Chinese wheat flour pancakes (or made from a mix)
small handful of toasted sesame seeds, to garnish

This makes a great light snack or supper or delicious party food. The meaty Chinese mushrooms add bite and texture, and the oyster sauce gives a rich umami flavor to the beef. Easy and quick—perfect for a lazy wok day!

If you are vegan, you can use small pieces of smoked tofu.

Serves 2 kcal 473 carbs 32.8g protein 41.6g fat 19.2g

Season the beef with the salt, white pepper, rice wine or dry sherry, and the oyster sauce, and rub in.

Heat a wok over high heat until smoking, add the canola oil, and give it a swirl. Add the beef, and fry for a few seconds until browned at the edges, then add the mushrooms, and toss for a few minutes until tender. Season with the tamari or light soy sauce and sesame oil, then sprinkle in the garlic chives or scallions. Transfer to a plate, cover, and keep warm.

Wipe out the wok, half-fill with water, and bring to a simmer. Place the wheat flour pancakes on a heatproof plate lined with greaseproof paper, then put on a rack set over the wok and steam for 4 minutes over high heat, then remove to warm plates and cover with foil.

Spoon some of the beef and mushroom mixture onto each pancake, garnish with toasted sesame seeds, and eat immediately.

PEARLY BEEF BALLS

½ cup glutinous rice
dried goji berries

For the beef balls
14oz ground beef
pinch of sea salt
pinch of ground white pepper
1 tablespoon Shaohsing rice wine
  or dry sherry
2oz French beans (thin green
  beans), finely diced
1 teaspoon vegetable bouillon
  powder
1 teaspoon toasted sesame oil
1 teaspoon cornstarch

For the dipping sauce
1 tablespoon Chinkiang black
  rice vinegar or balsamic
  vinegar
ginger matchsticks

Although this is quick to cook once everything is prepared, you first need to soak the glutinous rice for 1½ hours.

This is my variation of the Cantonese classic, which is usually made with pork instead of beef. But the Chinese use meat very sparingly and a little goes a long way! These delightful beauties are perfect when steamed. If you cannot get glutinous rice, use sushi rice instead.

Serves 2 kcal 488 carbs 32.8g protein 41.6g fat 19.2g

Wash the glutinous rice until the water runs clear, then soak in fresh cold water for 1 ½ hours. Drain.

Mix together all the ingredients for the beef balls. Shape the mixture into about 12 balls the size of small golf balls, then roll in the drained rice to coat and place in a bamboo steamer. Top each one with a goji berry, cover and steam over a wok over high heat for 15–20 minutes until the beef is cooked, and the rice is *al dente* but pearlescent.

Serve with the black rice vinegar dipping sauce, adding the ginger matchsticks to it.

10 mins

5 mins

GF DF

FIVE-SPICE PORK AND BLACK BEAN WOOD EAR WITH SCALLIONS

1 tablespoon canola oil

1-inch piece of ginger, peeled and grated

1 red chile, seeded and finely chopped

7oz pork fillet, sliced into ¼-inch strips, lightly dusted with cornstarch

pinch of Chinese five-spice powder

1 teaspoon dark soy sauce

1 tablespoon Shaohsing rice wine or dry sherry

3½oz dried wood ear mushrooms, (soaked in hot water for 10 minutes), sliced into strips, or canned bamboo shoots

1 teaspoon black bean paste

scant ½ cup hot vegetable stock

1 tablespoon tamari or low-sodium light soy sauce

1 tablespoon cornstarch, blended with 2 tablespoons cold water

2 scallions, sliced on the diagonal, to garnish

I'm a huge fan of dried Chinese wood ear mushrooms, which, when soaked, double in size and become a delicious crunchy addition to any stir fry. They are only available in Chinese food stores, but these days you can order anything online. They are so full of nutritious goodness, that my mother blends them into a smoothie-like drink—apparently their bouncy texture replicates collagen and is good for the skin (it also helps the digestion).

For vegans, substitute the pork with smoked tofu or a medley of meaty mushrooms. Enjoy!

Serves 2 kcal 370 carbs 42.8g protein 27.9g fat 10.8g

Heat a wok over high heat until smoking, add the canola oil, and give the oil a swirl. Add the ginger and chile, and toss for a few seconds, then add the pork, and sear on one side. Season with the five-spice powder, dark soy sauce, and rice wine or dry sherry, and cook for 1 minute until cooked through. Add the wood ear mushrooms or bamboo shoots, the black bean paste, vegetable stock, and tamari or light soy sauce, and bring the sauce to a boil. Stir in the blended cornstarch and quickly stir together (the cornstarch thickens quickly). Garnish with the scallions, and serve immediately with jasmine rice.

BEEF AND SPINACH RICE SOUP

1 tablespoon canola oil

1-inch piece of ginger, peeled and sliced into matchsticks

3½oz sirloin steak, finely diced

½ teaspoon dark soy sauce

pinch of Chinese five-spice powder

1 tablespoon Shaohsing rice wine or dry sherry

2 cups hot vegetable stock

1½ cups cooked jasmine rice

1 tablespoon tamari or low-sodium light soy sauce

pinch of ground white pepper

1–2 teaspoons toasted sesame oil

1 tablespoon cornstarch, blended with 2 tablespoons cold water

3½oz baby leaf spinach

1 scallion, finely sliced, to garnish

This quick and heart-warming dish starts off as a stir-fry, and then when you add cooked rice, veggie stock, and seasonings, it turns into a soupy congee, which is comfort food for me. You can make it chunkier by adding more rice and less stock, or if you like a brothy kind of dish, add more veggie stock. Either way, the wilted spinach will give you a delicious hit of green.

If you are vegan, replace the beef with mushrooms and smoked tofu.

Serves 2 kcal 315 carbs 37.4g protein 17.1g fat 12.1g

Heat a wok over high heat until smoking, add the canola oil, and give it a swirl. Add the ginger, and toss for a few seconds, then add the diced steak, and sear on one side. Flip the meat over, season with the dark soy sauce and five-spice powder, and cook for 1 minute. Add the rice wine or dry sherry, then pour in the hot vegetable stock, ½ cup boiling water, and the cooked jasmine rice. Season with the tamari or light soy sauce, white pepper, and sesame oil, then stir in the blended cornstarch, and bring to a boil. Stir in the baby spinach to wilt, then garnish with the scallion, and serve immediately.

10 mins

45 mins

DF

OXTAIL AND TURNIP NOODLE SOUP (NUOROMEIN)

2 tablespoons canola oil

5 whole baby shallots, peeled

18oz oxtail, chopped into 1-inch chunks

1 whole fat garlic clove, peeled

1 red chile, sliced

1-inch piece of ginger, peeled and left whole

1 star anise

½ daikon (6 inches), cut into 1-inch chunks

1 small carrot, sliced in half lengthwise, then cut into ¼-inch half-moon chunks

2½ cups chicken stock

1 tablespoon Shaohsing rice wine or dry sherry

1 tablespoon chili bean paste

1 teaspoon chili sauce

1 teaspoon dark soy sauce

2 teaspoons soft brown sugar

2 heads of baby bok choy, sliced down the middle

7oz dried flat wheat flour or udon noodles

For the garnish

2 scallions, sliced into strips and soaked in iced water for 5 minutes to curl, drained

small bunch of cilantro, stems and leaves, sliced

I love the warmth and comforting flavor of this broth, alongside the slippery wheat flour or udon noodles. It makes an easy and satisfying supper. For those who like a "cleaner" broth, blanch the oxtail in boiling water for 10 minutes before cooking to remove any impurities. But if you are short on time, a good wash beforehand should be enough.

Serves 2 kcal 752 carbs 83.3g protein 32.1g fat 8.9g

Heat a large wok over high heat, pour in 1 tablespoon of the canola oil, and give it a swirl. Add the baby shallots, and brown for less than 1 minute. Add the oxtail pieces, and brown each side for 30 seconds, then stir in the garlic, chile, ginger, star anise, daikon, and carrot. Pour in 1¼ cups water and the chicken stock, and season with the rice wine or dry sherry, the chili bean paste, chile sauce, dark soy sauce and soft brown sugar. Cover and simmer over medium heat for 45 minutes.

Bring a large pot of water to a boil, and blanch the bok choy for less than 30 seconds. Lift out, drain well, and set aside. Add the noodles to the boiling water, and cook according to the package instructions, then drain and dress with the remaining canola oil, and toss together well.

Before serving, check the seasoning of the broth, and add more soy sauce to taste, if preferred. Portion the noodles into two bowls, then divide the oxtail mixture between the bowls, and add the bok choy. Garnish with the scallions and cilantro, and serve immediately.

15 mins

5 mins

GF DF

CHUNKY BLACK PEPPER HONEY BEEF

18oz sirloin steak, cut into
    ¼-inch-thick cubes
pinch of sea salt
pinch of cracked black pepper
1 tablespoon tamari or low-
    sodium light soy sauce
small handful of cilantro leaves,
    to garnish

For the stir-fry
1 tablespoon canola oil
1 garlic clove, whole, peeled
2 large white onions, cut into
    ¼-thick inch chunks
1 tablespoon Shaohsing rice wine
    or dry sherry
2 red bell peppers, deseeded
    and cut into ¼-inch chunks

For the sauce
scant ½ cup cold chicken stock
1 tablespoon oyster sauce
1 tablespoon tamari or low-
    sodium light soy sauce
1 teaspoon dark soy sauce
4 tablespoons runny honey
½ teaspoon cracked black
    pepper
1 tablespoon cornstarch

This is super quick to make—you can have all the ingredients pre-prepped, and then just wok it up at the last minute so that it's piping hot. I promise you this will be a winner with your family and friends.

Serves 4 kcal 333 carbs 33.5g protein 32.1g fat 8.9g

Put the beef in a bowl with the sea salt, black pepper, and tamari or light soy sauce and mix well.

Put all the ingredients for the sauce into a small jug, and stir to mix well.

For the stir-fry, heat a wok over high heat until smoking, add the canola oil, and give the oil a swirl. Add the garlic, and cook for a few seconds, then add the onions, and stir-fry until translucent. Add the beef chunks, and sear on one side for 20 seconds, then flip the meat over, and cook to your liking (for best results cook to medium). Then season with the rice wine or dry sherry. Add the red bell peppers, and toss for 30 seconds until slightly softened. Remove the beef, onions, and red peppers and set aside on a plate.

Pour the sauce into the wok, and reduce until sticky. Quickly return the beef and vegetables to the wok, and gently toss together well. Garnish with the cilantro, and serve with jasmine rice and Garlic Wok Tossed Baby Bok Choy (see page 76).

CHING'S MACANESE MINCHI

20 mins

35 mins

DF

For the roasted oyster mushrooms

7oz oyster mushrooms

1–2 tablespoons olive oil

1–2 large pinches of sea salt

2 large pinches of cracked black pepper

2 large pinches of dried red pepper flakes

For the potatoes

2 cups sunflower oil

18oz baby potatoes, scrubbed, left unpeeled, and cut into 3/8-inch dice

For the pork

1 tablespoon canola oil

1 large white onion, diced

2 bay leaves

1 garlic clove, minced

18oz lean ground pork

1 tablespoon Shaohsing rice wine or dry sherry

1–2 tablespoons oyster sauce

1–2 tablespoons sweet soy sauce (Indonesian *kecap manis*)

1–2 tablespoons Worcestershire sauce

1 teaspoon dark soy sauce

pinch of ground white pepper (optional)

2 large scallions, sliced into 3/8-inch rounds, to garnish

>

contd overleaf

This is another dish that takes slightly longer to cook, but it's well worth the effort. Macanese *minchi* is traditionally wok-fried pork with some soy and fried potatoes, served with runny fried eggs on top—pure comfort food! It is utterly delicious when served with jasmine rice. I've gone a little step further and added oven-roasted mushrooms. It's so good, you'll want to have it every weekend.

For vegans, use textured vegetable protein (TVP) instead of ground pork, vegetarian oyster sauce instead of oyster sauce, and then just omit the fried eggs.

Serves 4 kcal 811 carbs 102g protein 44.8g fat 28.5g

Wash the rice until the water runs clear. Place in a medium saucepan, add the chicken stock and 1¼ cups water, and bring to a boil. Once the water is boiling, turn the heat to low, cover with a lid, and cook for 15–20 minutes until the rice is fluffy.

Meanwhile, preheat the oven to 350°F. Put the oyster mushrooms on a roasting pan, drizzle with the olive oil, and season with the salt, black pepper, and red pepper flakes. Place in the oven, and roast for 5–6 minutes, then remove. Turn the oven down to low, and return the mushrooms to keep warm.

To cook the potatoes, heat a wok or medium saucepan, add the sunflower oil, and heat to 350°F, or until a bread cube dropped in the oil turns golden brown in 15 seconds, and floats to the surface. Carefully lower the potato cubes into the oil, and fry for 5 minutes until crisp and golden on the edges and soft on the inside. (You may have to do this in batches.) Drain on paper towels. When all the potatoes are cooked, drain the last batch, and the oil into a steel colander set over a heatproof bowl. Keep the oil to use again.

Heat the wok again over high heat until smoking, add the canola oil, and give it a swirl. Fry the onion until translucent, then add the bay leaves and garlic, followed by the ground pork. Sear and brown the pork for 45 seconds, then stir-fry to cook it.

For the rice

2 cups jasmine rice

14oz chicken stock

For the fried eggs

1 tablespoon canola oil

4 eggs

pinch of salt

pinch of ground white pepper

Before the pork is completely cooked, add the rice wine or dry sherry, and season to taste with the oyster sauce, sweet soy sauce, Worcestershire sauce, and dark soy sauce. Add a pinch of ground white pepper here, if you like. Toss well until the seasoning has coated the pork. Add the fried potatoes, and toss together for 1 minute. Adjust the seasoning to taste, if desired, then transfer to a warmed plate and set aside.

Cook the eggs. Heat a frying pan, add the canola oil, and give it a swirl. Crack in the eggs, and fry over medium heat for 1 minute, until the bottoms are crispy, but the egg yolks are still runny on the top. Season with the salt and white pepper.

Remove the mushrooms from the oven.

Place some rice in the center of a large serving plate. Pour the ground pork and potato (*minchi*) over the top, arrange the mushrooms around the sides, and lay the fried eggs over the top. Garnish with a sprinkle of scallions and serve immediately.

Ching's Tip (optional)

Serve with some sliced raw red cabbage seasoned with lemon juice, salt, black pepper and olive oil.

10–12 mins

3 mins

DF

CHING'S CHAR SIU BACON AND SHRIMP RICE NOODLES

For the noodles

3 ½oz dried folded flat rice noodles

1 teaspoon toasted sesame oil

For the *char siu* bacon and brown shrimp topping

1 tablespoon canola oil

1 tablespoon peeled and grated ginger

3 ½oz beech-smoked thick-cut bacon, diced

1 tablespoon *char siu* (Chinese barbecue) sauce

1 teaspoon dark soy sauce

2 ½oz cooked baby brown shrimp

To serve and for the garnish

2 ½oz blanched bean sprouts

1 teaspoon tamari or low-sodium light soy sauce

1 teaspoon Oriental sesame dressing

2 scallions, finely chopped

Like all noodles, rice noodles have little flavor themselves, but one thing that makes them more delicious than other noodles (and write to me if you disagree) is that they are incredible at absorbing flavors—as in a delicious Pad Thai or Vietnamese Pho. In this recipe, they are served plain, but topped with a shrimpy-porky stir-fry, and bean sprouts and scallions—it makes the perfect quick dinner all year round, plus it's super healthy too.

Serves 2 kcal 404 carbs 50.2g protein 19.7g fat 14.7g

Bring 1 quart water to a boil in a pan, add the noodles, and cook for 10–12 minutes until *al dente*. Drain under cold water, drizzle the sesame oil over, and toss together to prevent the noodles from sticking. Set aside.

Meanwhile, heat a wok over high heat until smoking, add the canola oil, and give it a swirl. Add the ginger, and stir-fry for a few seconds, then add the diced thick-cut bacon, and cook for 2 minutes, until browning at the edges. Add the *char siu* sauce and toss for 30 seconds, then add the dark soy sauce, and cook for 30 seconds. Add the brown shrimps, and stir-fry for another 30 seconds.

To serve, place the noodles on a serving plate, top with the blanched bean sprouts, then drizzle on the tamari or light soy sauce and sesame dressing. Arrange the *char siu* bacon and shrimps on top, garnish with the scallions, and serve immediately.

10 mins

5 mins

+ 20 minutes to
cook the rice

GF DF

MACANESE-STYLE FRIED RICE—PORTUGUESE CHOURIÇO, BABY SCALLOPS, AND CILANTRO

7oz (generous 1 cup) jasmine rice
2 tablespoons vegetable oil
2 garlic cloves, minced
2 shallots, finely chopped
½ medium jalapeño chile,
seeded and finely chopped
3 small scallions, sliced into
⅜-inch rounds
2oz Portuguese black Iberian
chouriço or Spanish chorizo,
diced
4oz raw baby or bay scallops,
cleaned
1 tablespoon Shaohsing rice wine
or dry sherry
2–3 tablespoons tamari or low-
sodium light soy sauce
pinch of sea salt
pinch of ground white pepper
juice of 1 large lemon
small handful of cilantro leaves
and stems, sliced

The Macanese cuisine is a fusion of Portuguese and Chinese. The Portuguese way of making seafood rice is to cook it risotto-style so that the rich flavours of the ingredients, stock and spices infuse the rice, whereas the Chinese typically like fried rice. So I'm making Portuguese-Chinese fried rice using a classic Portuguese sausage, chouriço, made from Iberian black pigs. Much like the Spanish chorizo, it is peppered with paprika and other flavoursome spices. When cooked, it leaches a delicious, reddish, spicy oil that gets absorbed by the starchy rice. Sweet baby scallops are my seafood of choice here. This dish will have your guests wanting more.

Serves 4 kcal 315 carbs 45.3g protein 13.3g fat 11.3g

Place the rice in a strainer and wash until the water runs clear to rinse away the excess starch. Place the rice in a medium pot, add 1¾ cups water and bring to a boil. Once boiling, reduce the heat to low, cover the pan, and simmer for 15–20 minutes, until all the water has been absorbed and the rice is cooked through. Remove from the heat, and fluff up the grains, then, to reduce the moisture of the rice, transfer to a tray and fan out—this will ensure the rice is dry enough to make the fried rice.

Heat a wok over high heat until smoking, add the vegetable oil, and give it a swirl. Add the garlic, shallots, chile, and scallions, and stir for a few seconds. Add the diced chouriço or chorizo, and cook for 30 seconds to crisp the edges, then add the baby scallops and toss together for 15 seconds.. Season with the rice wine or dry sherry, then add the cooked rice to the wok, and mix well, so the rice absorbs all the flavors in the wok.

Season with the tamari or light soy sauce, sea salt, and white pepper, and toss well, so that all the rice is turned light brown. Add the lemon juice, and toss the cilantro through. Give it a final stir, then remove from the heat, transfer to serving bowls, and serve immediately.

15 mins

2–3 mins

DIRTY HOISIN CRANBERRY KIMCHI PORK HOT CHEESE SANDWICH

5oz pork loin, sliced thinly
    against the grain, on an angle
2 tablespoons canola oil
1 red onion, sliced into rings
pinch of soft brown sugar
1 tablespoon Shaohsing rice wine
    or dry sherry

For the marinade

1 garlic clove, finely grated
1 teaspoon runny honey
1 teaspoon tamari or low-sodium
    light soy sauce
1 teaspoon cranberry jam
1 tablespoon hoisin sauce
½ teaspoon sriracha chili sauce

Assemble with

2 thick slices white bread
spread of mayonnaise
spread of Dijon mustard
    (optional)
1 generous cup medium Cheddar
    cheese, grated
small handful of baby spinach
    leaves
2oz kimchi (Korean fermented
    cabbage), roughly chopped
½ tablespoon finely chopped
    scallions

My guilty pleasure since living in the UK is making naughty sandwiches. I love a hot sandwich and it's so comforting! This one is a mash-up of Chinese, Korean, and British influences. The result is a fruity, spicy, fermented, porky, savory hot sandwich—it all sounds so wrong, but it's so right. Ideally, you'd make the cranberry jam yourself, as store-bought can be on the sweet side, though you only need a bit of it. Serve with a fruity craft beer. Enjoy!

Serves 1 kcal 869 carbs 77.4g protein 50g fat 41.1g

Put all the ingredients for the marinade in a bowl, and stir to combine. Add the pork slices, and marinate for 10 minutes.

Heat a wok over medium heat, add 1 tablespoon of the canola oil, and give it a swirl. Wok-fry the onion with the sugar until caramelized, then spoon out onto a plate.

Heat the wok over medium-high heat, add the remaining oil, and give it a swirl. Add the marinated pork slices, season with the rice wine and stir-fry for 2 minutes until cooked through. Set aside.

Spread one slice of bread with mayonnaise, and the other with Dijon mustard, if you like. Top one slice with the cheese. Place the cheese-topped slice under a hot broiler for 1–2 minutes. Remove from the oven and place the spinach on top of the cheese. Then add the slices of pork and the caramelised red onion and sprinkle with the kimchi and scallion. Place the remaining bread slice on top, cut in half on the diagonal, and serve immediately.

SPICY FOUR-PEPPER LAMB

12oz boneless lamb loin, cut into
  cubes
pinch of sea salt
pinch of ground white pepper
1 teaspoon cornstarch
10 whole dried red chiles or
  small fresh arbol chiles
1 teaspoon Sichuan peppercorns
2 tablespoons canola oil
2 garlic cloves, minced
1-inch piece of ginger, peeled and
  coarsely chopped
1 small jalapeño, seeded and
  diced
1 green bell pepper, seeded and
  sliced lengthwise
1 star anise
2 tablespoons Chinkiang black
  rice vinegar or balsamic
  vinegar
1 tablespoon tamari or low-
  sodium light soy sauce
2–3 tablespoons chili oil, or to
  taste

Here, delicious, chunky lamb is wok-fried with Sichuan pepper,
whole dried chiles, ginger, jalapeño, star anise, and green
bell pepper. It's punchy, and layered with heat, perfect for
the spice lover. This is not a one-wok process—you cook the
spices, the lamb, and the peppers separately, and then bring
them all together, a method that my grandmother would
have followed, which ensures that every bit is wokked to
perfection. If you're feeling lazy, you can wok-fry the spices,
add the lamb, and then add the peppers and seasoning—it
will still be delish, and all will be forgiven. Perfect with
jasmine rice.

Serves 4 kcal 312 carbs 7.1g protein 17.9g fat 24.4g

Put the lamb into a bowl, add the salt, white pepper, and
cornstarch, and toss well to coat. Set aside for 5 minutes.

Heat a wok over medium heat until smoking, add the dried chiles
and Sichuan peppercorns, and toast, tossing continuously, until
fragrant and the chiles begin to blacken—about 10 seconds.
Transfer to a bowl, and reserve.

Reheat the wok over a medium heat until smoking, then add 1
tablespoon of the canola oil, and give the oil a swirl. Add the
lamb pieces to the wok in an even layer, and let them settle
for about 1 minute until they begin to brown. Then stir-fry the
lamb vigorously for about 3 minutes, until cooked through and
medium—well done on the inside. Transfer to a plate.

Reheat the wok, add the remaining tablespoon of canola oil, and
give it a swirl. Add the garlic, ginger, and jalapeño to the wok, and
stir-fry for 1 minute, until softened. Add the green bell pepper,
star anise, and toasted chiles and peppercorns, and toss until
the pepper is softened, about 2–3 minutes. Return the lamb to
the wok, and cook until very hot. Add the vinegar and tamari
or light soy sauce, and toss until well-combined. Add the chili
oil, and cook until heated through. Transfer to a large, shallow
serving plate, and serve immediately.

BEEF AND BLACK BEAN GREEN PEPPER NOODLES

For the beef

1 x 8oz ribeye steak, excess fat trimmed off, cut into ⅝-inch thick slices

1 teaspoon dark soy sauce

1 tablespoon cornstarch

1 red bird's eye chile, soaked in light soy sauce (to add a spicy edge to the dish), to garnish

For the rest of the stir-fry

2 tablespoons canola oil

2 garlic cloves, minced

1-inch piece of ginger, peeled and finely grated

1 red chile, seeded and finely chopped

1 teaspoon fermented salted black beans, rinsed and crushed (or store-bought black bean sauce)

1 tablespoon Shaohsing rice wine or dry sherry

2 green bell peppers, seeded, and cut into julienne strips

1 tablespoon tamari or low-sodium light soy sauce

⅔ cup hot vegetable stock

2 tablespoons cornstarch, blended with 4 tablespoons cold water

14oz cooked egg noodles

2 scallions, sliced on the diagonal

This is based on the traditional Cantonese Beef with Black Bean Noodles. *Dou-chi* (fermented salted black beans) is a popular ingredient used across Southern China—from Sichuan in the southwest (where it is used in dishes such as twice-cooked pork) to Canton in the southeast (where it appears in dishes such as steamed sea bass). It is made from soybeans that once dried and salted, turn black during the fermentation process. The beans have an extremely salty flavor, and are widely used in Chinese cookery—most famously to make black bean sauce. The ingredients that best complement this sauce are beef and green bell peppers. The green peppers have a fresh, raw bitter-peppery bite that adds a savory crunch, and cooked beef is deeply rich in umami, which enhances the salty black bean notes. This is a simple, quick stir-fry; the perfect midweek supper, which delivers on taste, and is very easy to make. Tender beef ribeye strips are sliced relatively thickly, seasoned with some dark soy, and wok-fried with aromatics, homemade black bean sauce, and cooked egg noodles. You can add other vegetables too. Red chiles stir-fried with the dish, gives a salty, spicy taste that is irresistible. If you are vegan, use chunky sliced smoked tofu instead of the beef, and follow the rest of the recipe, or if you are not a fan of tofu, use a combination of fresh shimeji mushrooms and sliced shiitake mushrooms.

Serves 2 kcal 735 carbs 97.4g protein 42.6g fat 22.1g

Season the beef with the dark soy sauce, and dust with the cornstarch.

Heat a wok over high heat until smoking, add the canola oil, and give it a swirl. Add the garlic, ginger, and chile, and stir-fry for a few seconds to release their aroma. Add the black beans (or black bean sauce), and toss for 10 seconds, then add the beef, and let it settle for about 10 seconds to brown the edges. Flip the beef over, and when it starts to turn brown, add the rice wine or dry sherry to enrich the natural sweet flavor of the beef.

Add the green bell peppers, and stir-fry for 1 minute, then season with the tamari or light soy sauce. Add the vegetable stock. and bring to a boil, then stir in the blended cornstarch to thicken the sauce. Stir in the cooked noodles, and toss together well, until all the ingredients are coated lightly in the sauce. Adjust the seasoning to taste, if necessary. Divide between two plates, garnish with the scallions for a fresh bite and the soy-soaked bird's eye chile, and serve immediately.

15 mins

8 mins

DF

PEANUT PORK SATAY RICE NOODLES

For the peanut sauce
1oz (⅓ cup) toasted peanuts
1½ bird's eye chiles, chopped
1 tablespoon fish sauce
1 tablespoon superfine sugar
1 teaspoon sesame oil
1 teaspoon chopped cilantro
juice of 2 limes

For the stir-fry
5oz dried Pad Thai rice noodles
1 tablespoon canola oil
1-inch piece of ginger, peeled,
    and sliced into coins
10oz pork fillet, cut into ⅜-inch
    thick slices
1 tablespoon Shaohsing rice wine
    or dry sherry
1 tablespoon dark soy sauce
3 ½oz bok choy, leaves
    separated, stalks sliced into
    1-inch pieces
1 carrot, sliced on the diagonal
3 baby corn, sliced on the
    diagonal
5oz snow peas
1 tablespoon tamari or low-
    sodium light soy sauce
1 cup roasted salted peanuts
2 scallions, sliced on the diagonal
    into 1-inch pieces

For the garnishes
pinch of dried chile flakes
1 lime, cut into 4 wedges
1 scallion, sliced on the diagonal
    into thin slices

This is my stir-fry noodle version of a popular Thai street food snack. The best thing about this dish is that the sauce is so flavorful, all you have to do is choose your favorite crunchy vegetables and stir-fry it all together. I have chosen bok choy leaves and stalks, carrot, baby corn, snow peas, and scallions—a perfect 5-a-day vegetable fix. Simple and delicious for a midweek supper. Wokky on!

Serves 2 kcal 793 carbs 83.5g protein 49.7g fat 28.9g

To make the peanut sauce, crush the peanuts in a pestle and mortar. Add the chiles, fish sauce, sugar, sesame oil, and cilantro, and mash together until a thin paste forms. Add the lime juice, and stir to mix well. Adjust the seasoning to taste, if necessary. Set aside.

Soak the noodles in warm water for 10 minutes, then drain.

Heat a wok over high heat until smoking, add the canola oil, and give it a swirl. Add the ginger, and stir-fry for a few seconds to release its aroma and flavor into the oil. Add the pork slices, and let them settle in the wok for a few seconds, then flip the meat over, and toss until colored and caramelized at the edges. As the pork starts to brown, add the rice wine or dry sherry, and the dark soy sauce.

Quickly add all the vegetables, and stir-fry for 1 minute. Add the peanut sauce and drained noodles, toss well, and cook for another minute, until all the ingredients are well-coated in the sauce. Remove from the heat, and season with the tamari or light soy sauce. Sprinkle in the peanuts, and give it one last toss.

To serve, divide the noodle mixture between two plates, add the chile flakes, lime juice and scallion slices, to garnish, and eat immediately.

SMOKY BACON SCALLOPS

7oz large, hand-dived scallops, cleaned
pinch of salt
pinch of ground white pepper
2 tablespoons canola oil
2-inch piece of ginger, peeled and grated
3½oz smoked thick-cut bacon, diced
2 tablespoons Shaohsing rice wine or dry sherry
¼ cup hot vegetable stock
1 tablespoon tamari or low-sodium light soy sauce
1 tablespoon cornstarch, blended with 2 tablespoons cold water
2 pinches of ground white pepper (to taste)
1 tablespoon toasted sesame oil
1 scallion, sliced thinly on the diagonal, to garnish

Scallops are a prized ingredient in Chinese cooking and symbolize wealth because of their resemblance to gold bullion. This is a great dish for a Chinese New Year party— the perfect sweetness of the scallops, paired with the smoky, salty bacon is brought together by your favorite Chinese condiments, giving a rich harmony of flavors.

Serves 2 kcal 406 carbs 11.2g protein 25.4g fat 28.2 g

Season the scallops with the salt and white pepper.

Heat a wok over high heat until smoking, add the canola oil, and give it a swirl. Add the ginger, and stir-fry very quickly for a few seconds, then add the seasoned scallops, and stir for a few seconds. Add the diced thick-cut bacon, and toss together for 1 minute, then add the rice wine or dry sherry. Pour in the hot vegetable stock, and season with the tamari or light soy sauce.

Cook for 15 seconds, bringing the sauce to a bubble, then add the blended cornstarch, and stir all the ingredients well to coat them in the thick sauce. Adjust the seasoning to taste with the white pepper, and sprinkle on the sesame oil and scallion.

Remove from the heat, transfer to a serving dish, and serve immediately, with steamed vegetables and brown or jasmine rice.

5 mins

5 mins

GF DF

SPICY SMOKED BACON BROCCOLINI

1 tablespoon canola oil

2 garlic cloves, minced

1-inch piece of ginger, peeled, and finely grated

2 dried red chiles, torn

6oz smoked thick-cut bacon, diced

2 tablespoons Shaohsing rice wine or dry sherry

1 large carrot, sliced in half lengthwise, then in half again lengthwise, then on the diagonal into 2-inch pieces

7oz broccolini, sliced on the diagonal into 1-inch pieces

2 tablespoons Chinkiang black rice vinegar or balsamic vinegar

1 tablespoon tamari or low-sodium light soy sauce

Even a little bit of bacon goes a very long way. I'm a huge fan of diced, smoked thick-cut bacon. It is full of flavor, and when you pair it with some Chinese seasonings, crunchy carrots, and broccolini, the results are fabulous. Quick, simple, and delicious every time.

Serves 2 kcal 360 carbs 13g protein 20.4g fat 25.5g

Heat a wok over high heat until smoking, add the canola oil, and give it a swirl. Add the garlic, ginger, and chile pieces, and toss for a few seconds. Quickly add the diced thick-cut bacon, and stir-fry for 1 minute until browned.

Add the rice wine or dry sherry, then add the carrot and broccolini, and cook, tossing for 1 minute. Season with the vinegar, and cook for 1 minute until the veggies are crisp, then add the light soy sauce. Toss together well, and serve immediately with jasmine rice.

SICHUAN PORK AND FRENCH BEANS

1 tablespoon canola oil

1-inch piece of ginger, peeled and grated

½ teaspoon toasted Sichuan peppercorns, left whole

1 red chile, seeded and finely chopped

5oz ground pork

1 tablespoon Shaohsing rice wine or dry sherry

1 teaspoon dark soy sauce

7oz French beans (thin green beans) , sliced into 2-inch rounds

1 teaspoon chili bean paste

1 tablespoon lemon juice

1 tablespoon Chinkiang black rice vinegar or balsamic vinegar

1 tablespoon tamari or low-sodium light soy sauce

1 tablespoon chili oil

1 teaspoon toasted sesame oil

large handful of cilantro, finely chopped

This is a great way to cook French beans, but make sure they are fresh—when you buy them, snap them in half. If they make a crunchy snap, you know they are at their best, and full of moisture and goodness. This dish may seem like a lot of ingredients, but most are seasonings from the pantry. Just toss the beans in hot oil with ginger, Sichuan pepper, chiles and layers of seasoning, and the dish is ready in minutes. This is a mini side dish that you would add as an accompaniment to rice and other dishes.

For vegans, substitute rehydrated textured vegetable protein (TVP) for the ground pork, or you can use diced rehydrated, dried Chinese mushrooms.

Serves 2 kcal 270 carbs 7.5g protein 23.4g fat 16.2g

Heat a wok over high heat until smoking, add the canola oil, and give it a swirl. Add the ginger, Sichuan peppercorns, and red chile, and toss for a few seconds. Add the ground pork, and toss for 1 minute to crisp the edges of the pork. Season with the rice wine or dry sherry, and add the dark soy sauce.

Add the French beans, and toss well, then add a small splash of cold water to create some steam, and stir-fry for 2–3 minutes until the beans are tender. Season with the chili bean paste, lemon juice, vinegar, tamari or light soy sauce, chili oil, and toasted sesame oil.

Remove from the heat, stir in the cilantro, and serve immediately with jasmine rice.

PORK, KIMCHI AND WATER CHESTNUT FRIED RICE

1 tablespoon canola oil

1-inch piece of ginger, peeled and grated

7oz ground pork

pinch of sea salt

1 tablespoon Shaohsing rice wine or dry sherry

8oz canned water chestnuts, drained and sliced

9oz store-bought kimchi, drained, but reserve 1 tablespoon liquid

2½ cups cooked jasmine rice

3oz enoki mushrooms, cut into ⅜-inch slices

2 tablespoons tamari or low-sodium light soy sauce

1 teaspoon clear rice vinegar or cider vinegar

1 teaspoon chili oil

1 teaspoon toasted sesame oil

2 pinches of ground white pepper

2 scallions, sliced on the diagonal, to garnish

I love my Asian fusion dishes, what I like to call Fusian—the combination of spicy, pungent kimchi stir-fried with crunchy water chestnuts, and tender sweet enoki mushrooms, makes for a delicious marriage in wok heaven. This unusual flavor combination is my invention, and makes a simple but beautiful dish, perfect for entertaining.

If you're vegan, you can substitute textured vegetable protein for the ground pork, and just follow the rest of the recipe.

Serves 2 kcal 473 carbs 58.7g protein 29.9g fat 14.3g

Heat a wok over high heat until smoking, add the canola oil, and give it a swirl. Add the ginger, and toss for a few seconds, then add the ground pork, and stir-fry for 1 minute until browned at the edges. Season with the salt, and rice wine or dry sherry. Add the water chestnuts, kimchi, and jasmine rice, and stir-fry for 1 minute, until the rice absorbs all the delicious flavors.

Add the enoki mushrooms, season with the tamari or light soy sauce, vinegar, chili oil, sesame oil, white pepper, and the reserved liquid from the kimchi. Toss gently together once more, then garnish with the scallions and serve.

10 mins

70 mins

pre-cook, 40 mins braise-cook

CHING'S BRAISED HONG SAO PORK

1½lb pork belly, rindless

2 tablespoons canola or peanut oil

1 tablespoon peeled and grated ginger

3 tablespoons Shaohsing rice wine or dry sherry

3 star anise

1 teaspoon whole Sichuan peppercorns

3 long whole dried red chiles

1 cup chicken stock

3fl oz dark soy sauce

3 tablespoons soft brown sugar

pinch of salt

Another slightly longer cooking time. Regional variations on Hong *Sao Rou*, or red-braised pork can be found across China. It is said to have been one of Chairman Mao's favorite dishes. Traditionally, belly pork pieces are cooked in a braising liquid of spices and sugar; the caramelized sugar imparting a rich brown color. However, dark soy sauce is a popular way to enhance the umami salty-sweet flavor, and I have used it in this dish. It adds depth and color, giving the braising liquid a deep, reddish shine. The resulting pork should be sweet, salty, and spiced, and the sauce thick and sticky. I have reduced the amount of sugar to keep it healthier, but you can add more if you prefer a sweeter taste. It is best served simply with some steamed jasmine rice, and stir-fried greens such as bok choy.

Serves 4 kcal 674 carbs 16.2g protein 49.1g fat 47g

Bring 1½ quarts of water to a boil in a large pan. Add the pork belly slices, and simmer over medium heat for 30 minutes. Remove the pork, and drain well, then pat dry with paper towels, and slice into ¾-inch chunks.

Heat a wok over medium heat, add the canola or peanut oil, and give it a swirl. Add the pork pieces, and brown for 2 minutes, then add the ginger, rice wine or dry sherry, the star anise, Sichuan peppercorns, dried chiles, chicken stock, dark soy sauce, brown sugar, and salt. Cover with a tight-fitting lid, and cook over medium heat for 45 minutes, until the liquid has reduced and thickened slightly, and is a glossy, reddish-brown color.

Remove from the heat (see tip) and serve with steamed jasmine rice, and stir-fried greens of your choice.

Ching's Tip

For a smooth cooked sauce, strain through a sieve and discard the whole spices, or you can just eat around them like the Chinese do!

BLACK PEPPER BACON PINEAPPLE FRIED RICE

1 tablespoon canola oil

1 inch piece of ginger, peeled and grated

5oz smoked thick-cut bacon, diced

1 teaspoon dark soy sauce

pinch of ground black pepper

6 large fresh shiitake mushrooms, sliced into 3/8-inch strips

2¼ cups cooked jasmine rice

2 tablespoons tamari or low-sodium light soy sauce

¾ cup finely diced fresh pineapple flesh

1–2 scallions, sliced on a deep diagonal, to garnish

To serve

sriracha chili sauce

a few lime wedges (optional)

Who doesn't love ham and pineapple pizza? Hawaiian is one of my favorite pizza flavors, and I can't get enough of it, so a bacon and pineapple fried rice is the next best thing. The black pepper helps to add a bit of heat and spice to complement the smokiness of the bacon, and the sweetness of the pineapple. For those who are skeptical about pineapple in fried rice, it's a staple dish, and hails from the Yunnan region in China.

If you're vegan, you can lose the bacon and instead wok-fry some rehydrated cubed dried Chinese mushrooms, which are a great textured, earthy-smoky substitute.

Serves 2 kcal 466 carbs 49g protein 8.9g fat 22.8g

Heat a wok over high heat until smoking, add the canola oil, and give it a swirl. Add the ginger, and stir-fry for 5 seconds, then add the diced bacon, and stir-fry for 1 minute to caramelize it around the edges. Season with the dark soy sauce and black pepper, and toss well. Add the mushrooms and wok-fry together for 30 seconds.

Tip in the cooked rice, season with the tamari or light soy sauce, then add the pineapple, and stir gently to mix well. Garnish with the scallions, and serve with some sriracha chili sauce. For an extra zing, and a truly tropical taste, you can squeeze some lime juice over, if you like.

15 mins

8–9 mins

DF

PORKY SAUSAGE POT-STICKER DUMPLINGS

10½oz breakfast link sausages, skinned

2oz broccolini, stems only (reserve the heads for a wok-fry), blanched in boiling water for 10 seconds, drained and sliced into 2-inch rounds

2 scallions, finely sliced, to garnish

For the wrappers

1 package wheat flour *gyoza* wrappers

1 tablespoon all-purpose flour, plus extra for sprinkling

1 egg, beaten

1 tablespoon canola or vegetable oil

For the dipping sauce

2 tablespoons HP Brown Sauce

2 tablespoons sweet chili sauce

2 tablespoons tamari or low-sodium light soy sauce

Pot-stickers are so-named because they sometimes stick to the bottom of the wok. Adding a flour-water mix gives them a crispy coating on the bottom. You can make a large batch, freeze them, and cook straight from frozen. For a vegan version, substitute some finely chopped smoked tofu, and some lightly mashed fresh tofu for the sausages in the filling.

Makes 10 kcal 141 carbs 11.6g protein 7.1g fat 7.4g

Lay out the wrappers on a wooden board sprinkled with a little all-purpose flour. Spoon 2 teaspoons of the sausage meat onto each, and top with some broccolini stems. Seal the edges using a brush dipped into the beaten egg, then squeeze tight.

Heat a large, nonstick, shallow wok, add the canola or vegetable oil, and give it a swirl. Add the dumplings (making sure they don't touch each other), and cook for 30–45 seconds, until the base is golden and crispy (they should lift up easily).

Meanwhile, working quickly, measure 1 cup water into a jug, add 1 tablespoon all-purpose flour, and whisk until most of the lumps are gone. Pour over the dumplings, cover, and cook over low–medium heat for 3–4 minutes, until all the water has evaporated. Resist the temptation to remove the lid before the tops of the dumplings have a chance to cook through. Make sure the heat is not too hot, or the bottom of the dumplings will burn. However, if it is too low, the dumplings will go soggy, and you risk some of them sticking. So, keep an eye on them—it helps to have a glass lid, so you can gauge if the floured water is on a gentle simmer.

Meanwhile, combine all the ingredients for the dipping sauce in a bowl, and set aside.

Gently remove the dumplings from the wok (the flour water will have turned into a crispy and delicate flour sheet, and should break easily when lifting the dumplings out of the wok). Arrange on a serving plate, and drizzle with the dipping sauce, then garnish with the scallions, and serve immediately.

15 mins

5 mins

GF DF

CRISPY CHILI BEEF QUICK CHEAT "CONGEE"

10oz sirloin steak, fat removed, finely sliced into matchstick strips
2 tablespoons cornstarch
2½ cups sunflower oil

For the sauce
2 tablespoons tamari or low-sodium light soy sauce
2 tablespoons sweet chili sauce
juice of 1 small orange

For the quick cheat congee
2¼ cups cooked jasmine rice
2⅓ cups hot vegetable stock
1 tablespoon tamari or low-sodium light soy sauce
1 teaspoon toasted sesame oil
pinch of ground white pepper

To serve
1 carrot, cut into julienne strips
2 scallions, finely sliced lengthwise
chili oil (optional)

This combines two of my favorite comfort foods into one dish—comforting "congee" (although a quick cheat version) and crispy chili beef. The result is one helluva addictive dish!

If you're vegan, you can use fried strips of tofu, or sliced fresh shiitake mushrooms.

Serves 2 kcal 583 carbs 72.2g protein 41.8g fat 16.3g

Put all the ingredients for the congee in a medium pan, add a scant ½ cup boiling water, mix well and bring to a simmer, then keep on low-medium heat.

For the crispy beef, dip the beef strips in the cornstarch, and shake off any excess. Place on a plate. Heat a wok over high heat, and fill to a third of its depth with the sunflower oil. Heat the oil to 350°F, or until a cube of bread turns golden brown in 15 seconds and floats to the surface. Deep-fry the beef until golden, then drain on paper towels.

While the beef is draining, make the sauce. Heat a small wok, add the tamari or light soy sauce, sweet chili sauce, and orange juice, and cook until thickened. Add the beef strips, and toss until they're all coated in the sauce.

To serve, divide the congee between two bowls, dress each with some julienned carrot, then top with crispy chili beef and sprinkle on the scallions. If you like, spoon some chili oil around the edges, then serve immediately.

MISO HONEY RIBS

21oz pork ribs, chopped into 1¼–
1½-inch lengths
sunflower oil, for shallow-frying
1 scallion, sliced on the diagonal
into thin slices, to garnish

For the marinade
pinch of sea salt
pinch of ground white pepper
1 tablespoon red miso paste
1 tablespoon tamari or low-
sodium light soy sauce
1 tablespoon mirin (Japanese
rice wine)

For the sauce
2 garlic cloves, minced
2 tablespoons mirin
1 tablespoon red miso paste
2 tablespoons tamari or low-
sodium light soy sauce
1 tablespoon soft brown sugar
1 tablespoon runny honey

This is perfect party finger food. Marinating the ribs in red miso paste for 20 minutes, means the flavors get absorbed before you wok-fry them.

If you're vegan, you can make large, chunky, tofu dippers, and then follow the rest of the recipe, frying the tofu until golden, and substitute the honey for golden syrup.

Serves 4 kcal 415 carbs 15.7g protein 29.2g fat 26.1g

Put all the ingredients for the marinade into a large bowl, and stir to combine. Add the pork ribs, and turn to coat, then cover the bowl, and leave to marinate for at least 20 minutes, or for as long as possible, in the fridge.

Meanwhile, combine all the ingredients for the sauce in a bowl, and set aside.

Heat a wok over high heat until smoking, then fill to a quarter of its depth with sunflower oil. Heat the oil to 350°F, or until a cube of bread turns golden brown in 15 seconds and floats to the surface. Using a spider, carefully lower half the ribs into the oil, and shallow-fry until cooked through and browned.

Lift the ribs out of the wok with the spider, and drain on paper towels. Repeat with the other half. Drain the wok of oil through a heatproof colander into a heatproof bowl, and wipe it clean, then reheat over high heat.

Add the sauce to the wok, and cook over low-medium heat for 5–6 minutes, until the sauce has reduced to a sticky consistency. Toss the ribs back in and stir to coat. Garnish with the scallion, and serve immediately.

10 mins

5 mins

GF DF

FIVE-SPICE PORK WITH BABY PAK CHOY

2 tablespoons canola oil

2 pinches of sea salt

2 garlic cloves, crushed

1-inch piece of ginger, peeled and finely chopped

1 teaspoon Chinese five-spice powder

9oz sliced pork loin

1 tablespoon Shaohsing rice wine or dry sherry

1 tablespoon tamari or low-sodium light soy sauce

1 teaspoon dark soy sauce

7oz baby bok choy, leaves separated

¼ cup hot vegetable stock

1 teaspoon cornstarch, blended with 1 tablespoon cold water

This is a straightforward, home-style Chinese dish. It can be varied in lots of ways, but I love the simplicity of Chinese Five-spice, ginger, rice wine, and soy—these are the flavors I call comfort and "home."

To make this one vegan, lose the pork, and substitute with meaty oyster mushrooms.

Serves 2 kcal 411 carbs 7.5g protein 35.6g fat 26.6g

Heat a wok over high heat until smoking, add the canola oil, and give it a swirl. Add the salt, garlic, ginger, and five-spice, and cook for a few seconds. Add the pork slices, and let them settle in the wok for a few seconds, then flip the meat over, and toss until colored and caramelized at the edges. As the pork starts to brown, add the rice wine or dry sherry, and cook until evaporated. Season with the light and dark soy sauces. Add the bok choy, and toss together for 1 minute until the leaves have wilted. Add the hot vegetable stock, bring to a bubble, then stir in the blended cornstarch and cook briefly. Give it a final toss, and remove the wok from the heat. Transfer to serving plates, and serve immediately.

PORK, GINGER AND DUCK EGG CONGEE

5 mins

33 mins

DF

1 quantity Classic Plain Congee "Zhou" (see page 52)

2 "thousand-year-old" duck eggs, sliced into eighths

1 tablespoon canola oil

1-inch piece of ginger, peeled and finely sliced

7oz pork fillet, finely sliced

1 tablespoon Shaohsing rice wine, dry sherry, or vegetable stock

3 fresh shiitake mushrooms, rinsed, patted dry, and finely diced

2 tablespoons tamari or low-sodium light soy sauce

pinch of sea salt

pinch of ground white pepper

dash of sesame oil (optional)

2 scallions, sliced on the diagonal

fried dough bread sticks, store-bought, sliced into ¼-inch rounds, to serve (optional)

This is a variation on the Classic Congee recipe on page 52, and one of my favorite breakfasts. The famous *cha chaan teng* cafés in Hong Kong (especially the ones located in the old wet market at Canton Road in Kowloon) sell similar steaming bowls of pork, ginger, and duck egg congee. My aunt would go shopping early for ingredients in the wet market, and then reward herself with a steaming bowl of this congee—it's so comforting.

Serves 4 kcal 342 carbs 43.7g protein 21g fat 10.5g

Make the congee as directed on page 52, then 5 minutes before the full cooking time, add the duck egg pieces.

Heat a separate wok over high heat until smoking, add the canola oil. and give it a swirl. Add the ginger, and stir quickly, then add the pork slices, and stir quickly. Add the rice wine, dry sherry, or vegetable stock, and the diced mushrooms. Season with the tamari or light soy sauce.

Add the ginger pork stir-fry to the congee, and stir in well. Season the congee with the salt and white pepper. Add a dash of sesame oil, if you like, and sprinkle on the sliced scallions. Serve with bread stick slices, if you have some. Yum!

SICHUAN BACON AND LEEK WOK-FRY

1 tablespoon canola oil

1 garlic clove, crushed

1 teaspoon whole Sichuan
   peppercorns

5oz smoked thick-cut bacon,
   diced

1 tablespoon Shaohsing rice wine
   or dry sherry

2 baby leeks, cut at a 45° angle
   into 2-inch slices

1 tablespoon tamari or low-
   sodium light soy sauce

1 tablespoon Chinkiang black
   rice vinegar or balsamic
   vinegar

1 teaspoon chili oil

½ teaspoon toasted sesame oil

Mmm... bacon and leek. Such a great combo, particularly in this smoky, Sichuan-inspired stir-fry. It's my cheat go-to when I want the flavors of the classic Sichuan twice-cooked pork, but a quicker, speedier fix. Perfect with jasmine rice.

If you're vegan, use smoked tofu instead of the smoked bacon.

Serves 2 kcal 283 carbs 4.1g protein 13.4g fat 23.7g

Heat a wok over high heat until smoking, add the canola oil, and give it a swirl. Add the garlic and Sichuan peppercorns, and toss for a few seconds. Add the diced bacon, and stir-fry for 3 minutes until caramelized at the edges, then add the rice wine or dry sherry. Add the leeks, and toss for 1 minute, adding a small dash of water around the edge of the wok to help create some steam. Once the leeks are wilted, season with the tamari or light soy sauce, vinegar, chili oil, and sesame oil. Serve immediately with plain jasmine rice.

5 mins

3 mins

DF

SOY MISO BEEF WITH SICHUAN PICKLE AND ZUCCHINI

14oz ribeye steak, cut into
¾-inch chunky slices
1 teaspoon cornstarch

For the marinade
1 tablespoon red miso paste
1 tablespoon soft brown sugar
1 tablespoon tamari or low-
sodium light soy sauce
1 teaspoon dark soy sauce
1 garlic clove, minced
1-inch piece of ginger, peeled and
finely grated

For the stir-fry
2 tablespoons canola oil
3 ½oz baby zucchini, cut on a
deep angle into ⅜-inch slices
1 tablespoon Shaohsing rice wine
or dry sherry
3oz Sichuan pickled mustard
stems in chili oil, drained and
cut into strips

For the garnish
1 fresh red cayenne chile pepper,
finely sliced into rings (seed, if
you like)
1 teaspoon toasted sesame
seeds

This is a juicy ribeye steak stir-fry with tons of flavor in which I fuse two ingredients—rich Japanese red miso, and pungent Sichuan pickled mustard stems in chili oil. Both are strong flavors, but there's no clash here—it's a great Asian fusion wok-fry! The chile adds a super delicious heat and spice, and the miso brings the deep savory notes. Delicious and perfect served with jasmine rice.

If you're vegan, substitute large meaty Portobello mushrooms for the steak.

Serves 2 kcal 494 carbs 18.3g protein 46.7g fat 26.2g

Place the beef in a shallow container. To make the marinade, pour ¼ cup cold water into a jug. Add the miso paste, and stir well to dissolve. Stir in the sugar, and light and dark soy sauces. Add the garlic and ginger, and stir well to combine, using a whisk. Pour this marinade over the beef, and leave for 5 minutes.

Heat a wok over high heat until smoking, add the canola oil, and give it a swirl. Dust the marinated beef with cornstarch, and place together with the marinade into the wok, and sear on one side for 30 seconds. Flip it over. For rare steak, cook for 30 seconds, for medium, toss for another minute, or for well-done, cook for 1¼ minutes.

Add the zucchini, and cook for another 30 seconds, then season with the rice wine or dry sherry, and cook until evaporated. Add the pickled mustard stems, and toss well to combine.

Garnish with the chile rings and sesame seeds, and serve with jasmine rice.

15 mins

3-4 mins

DF

OYSTER SAUCE BEEF AND BROCCOLINI

1 tablespoon canola oil

3 garlic cloves, minced

1-inch piece of ginger, peeled and grated

1 red cayenne chile pepper, sliced

1 sirloin steak, excess fat trimmed off, cut into 3/8-inch slices

1 tablespoon Shaohsing rice wine or dry sherry

9oz broccolini, sliced on the diagonal into 1-inch pieces

1 tablespoon dark soy sauce

large handful of bean sprouts

2 tablespoons tamari or low-sodium light soy sauce

2 tablespoons oyster sauce

Oyster sauce and beef are the perfect partners for each other! Oyster sauce is so rich and savory, it brings out the naturally occurring glutamates in the beef, which gives it that want-more savory quality. And beef and broccolini are also great together—the meaty soft goodness of the beef marries well with the crunchy sweet florets and stems of the broccolini. A match made in heaven, and made complete when served with jasmine rice or noodles.

If you are vegan, substitute chunky cubes of fried tofu, and a handful of fresh shiitake mushrooms for the beef. You can also substitute vegetarian oyster sauce (available in Chinese supermarkets or online) for the oyster sauce.

Serves 2 kcal 274 carbs 12.5g protein 31.9g fat 11.1g

Heat a wok over high heat until smoking, add the canola oil, and give it a swirl. Quickly add the garlic, ginger, and chile, and stir-fry a few seconds. Add the beef, and stir-fry for a few seconds.

As the beef starts to brown, add the rice wine or dry sherry, and follow quickly with the broccolini. Stir-fry together for 30 seconds, then add the dark soy sauce and toss well.

Add the bean sprouts, and toss together, then season with the tamari or light soy sauce and oyster sauce. Stir-fry for less than 1 minute, then serve immediately.

5 mins

3-4 mins

GF DF

DOFU RU LAMB WITH GAI LAN

For the broccoli stir fry
1 tablespoon canola oil
pinch of sea salt
³⁄₈-inch piece of ginger, peeled
   and sliced into matchsticks
1 small bird's eye red chile, sliced
12oz *gai lan* (Chinese broccoli) or
   broccoli
1 tablespoon Shaohsing rice wine
   or dry sherry

For the lamb stir fry
1 tablespoon canola oil
2 small garlic cloves, roughly
   chopped
7oz lamb neck fillet, cut on the
   diagonal into ³⁄₈-inch slices

For the sauce
1 tablespoon Shaohsing rice wine
   or dry sherry
1 cube *dofu ru* (fermented
   soybean curd)
1 tablespoon tamari or low-
   sodium light soy sauce
¼ cup cold stock
1 teaspoon cornstarch
pinch of soft brown sugar
pinch of cracked black pepper

This is an easy home-wokked lamb dish. Delicious and simple. Serve with wok-fried Chinese broccoli and jasmine rice.

Serves 2 kcal 347 carbs 10.6g protein 29.3g fat 21.2g

Mix all the ingredients for the sauce in a jug and stir well, using a whisk.

For the broccoli stir fry, heat a wok over high heat until smoking, add the canola oil, and give it a swirl. Add the salt, then the ginger and chile, and stir-fry for a few seconds. Add the *gai lan* or broccolini and stir-fry for 1 minute. Season with the rice wine or dry sherry, and stir-fry for another 2 minutes. Spoon out onto warm serving plates.

For the lamb, reheat the wok until smoking, add the canola oil, and give it a swirl. Add the garlic, and toss for a few seconds, then add the lamb. Leave to settle for a few seconds, then stir-fry until almost cooked. Add the sauce, bring to a bubble, and cook until the sauce has reduced to a sticky consistency. Spoon out on top of the *gai lan* and serve immediately.

30 mins

10 mins

DF

PORK AND CHINESE CABBAGE "SHUI-JIAO" —BOILED DUMPLINGS

7oz Napa cabbage stalks, finely diced
½ cup finely diced carrots
2 teaspoons sea salt
1 garlic clove, grated
thumb-sized knob of ginger, peeled and finely grated
10oz ground lean pork
1 vegetable stock cube, grated
2½ teaspoons superfine sugar
pinch of white pepper
dash of Shaohsing rice wine or dry sherry
dash of toasted sesame oil
1 oz scallions, finely diced
12 store-bought fresh square wheat flour dumpling wrappers
1 scallion, sliced into strips and soaked in ice water for 5 minutes to curl, drained, to garnish

For the dipping sauce
3 tablespoons toasted sesame oil
3 tablespoons tamari or low-sodium light soy sauce
3 tablespoons clear rice vinegar or cider vinegar
1 teaspoon sriracha chili sauce
1 red chile, seeded and finely chopped
few sprigs of cilantro, roughly chopped

Dumplings symbolize prosperity, so are perfect to welcome in Chinese New Year. If there are any left at the end of the meal (which I doubt!), they can be refreshed in boiling water, or fried in a lightly oiled, nonstick pan for a crispy coating. Enjoy!

Makes 12 kcal 98 carbs 8.7g protein 6.8g fat 4.1g*

Place the cabbage stalks and carrots in a bowl. Rub the salt into the vegetables, cover the bowl, and leave in the fridge for about 30 minutes. After 30 minutes, squeeze-dry the vegetables using your hands, and discard the water.

Combine all the ingredients for the dipping sauce in a bowl and set aside.

Add the garlic, ginger, and ground pork to the vegetables, season with the stock cube, sugar, white pepper, rice wine or dry sherry, sesame oil, and diced scallions, and mix well using your hands. Throw the mixture in the bowl a few times to aerate the filling, then gather into a large ball—it should come together like a dough, and not be overly sticky.

Spoon 1½ teaspoons of the mixture into the center of a dumpling wrapper. Dip your finger into a small bowl of water and run it along the edges of the wrapper. Fold and pleat the edges, pinching them well, until the edges are firmly sealed. Repeat with the remaining filling and wrappers.

Once all the dumplings have been folded and sealed, drop them into a wok of boiling water. Return to a boil, then turn the heat down to a simmer, and cook the dumplings for 3–4 minutes. The dumplings are cooked when they all float to the surface.

Remove the dumplings with a large slotted spoon, drain well, and place on a serving plate. Garnish with sliced fresh scallion curls and serve with the spicy dipping sauce.

*per dumpling

Glossary

Bamboo shoots
These add a crunchy texture to dishes. Boiled bamboo sprouts are also pickled in brine, giving them a sour taste, and in chiie oil, which gives them a spicy taste.

Bok choy
A vegetable with broad green leaves, which taper to white stalks. Crisp and crunchy, it can be boiled, steamed, or stir-fried.

Buckwheat Noodles
Made from 100% buckwheat flour, they contain nutrients such as protein, complex carbohydrates, and thiamine and manganese. They are also gluten- and fat-free.

Chili bean paste
Made from fava beans and chiles that have been fermented with salt to give a deep brown-red sauce. Some versions include fermented soybeans or garlic. Good in soups and braised dishes, it should be used with caution, as some varieties are extremely hot.

Chili oil
A fiery, orange-red oil made by heating dried red chiles in oil. To make your own, heat peanut oil in a wok, add dried red pepper flakes with seeds, and cook for 2 minutes. Remove from the heat, and leave the chile to infuse in the oil until completely cooled. Decant into a glass jar, and store for a month before using. For a clear oil, pass through a strainer.

Chili sauce/chili garlic sauce
A bright red, hot sauce made from chiles, vinegar, sugar, and salt. Some varieties are flavored with garlic and vinegar.

Chinese celery
Chinese celery stalks are slimmer and more tender than the Western variety and the flavor is more intense. Both the stalks and leaves are used.

Chinese leaf/Napa cabbage
This has a delicate, sweet aroma with a mild flavor that disappears when cooked. The white stalk has a crunchy texture, and remains succulent even after prolonged cooking. The Koreans mainly use it for kimchi.

Chinese chives (garlic chives)
Long, flat, green leaves with a strong garlic flavor. There are two varieties; one has small yellow flowers at the top, which can be eaten. Both are delicious.

Chinese five-spice powder
A blend of five spices—cinnamon, cloves, Sichuan peppercorns, fennel, and star anise—that give the distinctive sour, bitter, pungent, sweet, and salty flavors of Chinese cooking. This spice works extremely well with meats and in marinades.

Chinese sesame paste
Made from crushed roasted white sesame seeds blended with toasted sesame oil, it is used with other sauces to flavor dishes. If you cannot find it, you can use tahini instead, but it is a lot lighter in flavor so you will need to add more toasted sesame oil.

Chinese wood ear mushrooms
Dark brown-black fungi with ear-shaped caps. Very crunchy in texture, they do not impart flavor, but add color and crispness. They should be soaked in hot water for 20 minutes before cooking—they will double in size.

Chinkiang black rice vinegar
A strong aromatic vinegar made from fermented rice. The taste is mellow and earthy, and it gives dishes a wonderful smoky flavor. Balsamic vinegar makes a good substitute.

Choi sum
A green, leafy vegetable with a thick stem and tender leaves that belongs to the Brassica family, it is delicious steamed or stir-fried. Broccolini is a good substitute.

Cinnamon stick/bark
The dried bark of various trees in the *Cinnamomum* family. It can be used in pieces, or ground. Ground adds a sweet, woody fragrance.

Congee
Plain soupy rice porridge that can be combined with other ingredients, such as salted peanuts, fermented bean curd, and chile-pickled bamboo shoots.

Daikon (white radish)
Resembling a large white carrot, this crunchy vegetable has a peppery taste, and pungent smell, and is eaten raw, pickled, or cooked. It contains vitamin C and diastase, which aids digestion.

Dofu/fresh bean curd – Described as the "cheese" of China, this is made from soybean curd, and is quite bland, but takes on the flavor of whatever ingredients it is cooked with. Called tofu in Japan and dofu in Chinese, it is high in protein, and also contains B vitamins, isoflavones and calcium. Available as firm, soft, and silken, the firm variety is great in soups, salads and stir-fries. Silken has a cream cheese-like texture. *Dofu gan* is dried firm smoked beancurd.

Dried Chinese mushrooms
These need to be soaked in hot water for 20 minutes before cooking. They have a strong aroma, and a slightly salty taste, and therefore complement savory dishes well.

Egg noodles
Made from egg yolk, wheat flour, and salt, and available fresh or dried, these are come in a variety of thickness and shapes—flat and thin, long and rounded like spaghetti, and flat and coiled in a ball.

Enoki mushrooms
Tiny, white, very thin, long-stemmed mushrooms with a delicate flavor. Used raw, they add texture to salads. Lightly steamed, they are slight chewy.

Fermented salted black beans
Small black soybeans preserved in salt, which must be rinsed in cold water before use. They are used to make black bean sauce.

Fermented yellow bean paste
Made from yellow soybeans, water and salt. A cheat substitute would be hoisin sauce, though this is sweeter, and not as salty.

Fish sauce
A light amber liquid extracted from fermented fish and sea salt. The first press—made without additives or sugar—is the most prized.

Gai lan (Chinese broccoli)
Unlike Western green broccoli, *gai lan* comes in several varieties, some with yellow flowers, though most have large, glossy blue-green leaves with long, thick and crisp chunky stems. A good substitute is broccolini.

Goji berry (Chinese wolfberry)
The deep red, dried fruit of an evergreen shrub. Similar to a raisin, it is sweet and nutritionally rich, and can be eaten raw or cooked.

Hoisin sauce
Made from fermented soybeans, sugar, vinegar, star anise, sesame oil, and red rice, this is great used as a marinade, and as a dipping sauce.

Jasmine rice
A long-grain white rice originating from Thailand that has a nutty, jasmine-scented aroma. You need to rinse it before cooking until the water runs clear, to get rid of any excess starch.

Kaffir lime leaves
The leaves of the citrus fruit native to tropical Asia. The leaves emit an intense citrus aroma.

Kimchi
A Korean staple made from salted and fermented Chinese cabbage mixed with Korean radish, Korean dried chili flakes, scallions, ginger, and *geotgal* (salted seafood).

Lemongrass (citronella root)
A tough, lemon-scented stalk popular in Thai and Vietnamese cuisines. Look for lemon-green stalks that are tightly formed, firm, and heavy, with no bruising, tapering to a deeper green toward the end.

Mock duck
A vegetarian ingredient made from wheat gluten, soya, sugar, salt, and oil. A good substitute is bean curd or tofu skin.

Mirin
A sweet Japanese rice wine similar to sake, with a lower alcohol content, but a higher sugar one (the sugar occurs naturally as a result of the fermentation process).

Miso paste
A thick Japanese paste made from fermented rice, barley, soybeans, salt, and a fungus called *kojikin*. Sweet, earthy, fruity, and salty, it comes in many varieties, depending on the types of grains used.

Mung bean noodles
Made from the starch of green mung beans and water, these noodles come in various thicknesses, vermicelli being the thinnest. To use, soak in hot water for 5–6 minutes before cooking. If using in soups or deep-frying, no pre-soaking is necessary. They become translucent when cooked.

Mushroom oyster sauce – see oyster sauce

Nori (dried seaweed)
Sold in thin sheets, this is usually roasted over a flame until it turns black or purple-green. Used as a garnish or to wrap sushi, once opened, a pack must be sealed and stored in an airtight container or it loses its crispness. If this happens, just roast the sheets over an open flame for a few seconds until crisp.

Oyster mushrooms
Soft and chewy with a slight oyster taste, this white, yellow, or grey oyster-shaped fungi is moist and fragrant.

Oyster sauce
A seasoning sauce made from oyster extract that can also be used as a marinade. A vegetarian variety is also available. It is very salty, so taste the dish before adding.

Pad Thai noodles
Flat noodles, ½-inch wide, made from rice. They need to be soaked in hot water for 5 minutes before cooking.

Panko bread crumbs
Made from bread without crusts, these Japanese bread crumbs have a crisp texture.

Potato flour
A smooth, gluten-free flour made from potatoes that are steamed, dried, and then ground. It gives wonderful crispness when used to coat ingredients before frying.

Red miso paste — see Miso paste

Rice vinegar
A clear (white), mild vinegar made from fermented rice. Cider vinegar can be used as a substitute. Chinese black rice vinegar is a rich, aromatic vinegar that is used in braised dishes and sauces, and with noodles. When cooked, it gives a smoky flavor with a mellow and earthy taste. Balsamic vinegar makes a good substitute.

Sake
A fermented Japanese drink made from polished rice that is brewed in a similar way to wine. Its alcohol content ranges from 15–20%.

Sesame seeds
These oil-rich seeds add a nutty taste, and a delicate texture to many Asian dishes. Available in black, white/yellow and red varieties, toasted, and untoasted.

Shaohsing rice wine
Made from rice, millet, and yeast that has been aged for 3–5 years, it takes the "odor" or "rawness" out of meats and fish, and gives a bittersweet finish. Dry sherry makes a good substitute.

Shiitake mushrooms
These large, nutrient-rich, dark brown umbrella-shaped fungi are prized for their culinary and medicinal properties. When dried, they need to be soaked in water for 20 minutes before cooking.

Shimeji (beech) mushrooms
These come in white or brown varieties, and are characterized by long stems and tight concave caps.

Shrimp paste
A dry, smooth paste made by adding salt to shrimp or fish broth, which is then stored overnight, drained, and sun-dried. The mixture is then ground, and left to ferment in an earthenware jar. A good paste should be dark, deep purple.

Sichuan peppercorns
Known as "Hua jiao" in Mandarin or "flower pepper", these have a pungent, citrusy aroma. They can be wok-roasted, cooked in oil to flavor the oil, or mixed with salt.

Soy sauce
Made from wheat and fermented soybeans, soy sauce is available in dark and light varieties. Dark soy sauce is aged a lot longer than the light variety, and is mellower and less salty. Light soy sauce is used in China instead of salt. Wheat-free varieties, called tamari, are available, though it is quite salty. You can also buy low-sodium varieties.

Sriracha chili sauce
A hot sauce made from chile peppers, distilled vinegar, garlic, salt, and sugar. It is named after the coastal town of Si Racha, Eastern Thailand.

Star anise
The fruit of a small evergreen plant, these are called bajio or "eight horns" in Chinese. They have a distinct aniseed flavor, and are one of the ingredients found in Chinese five-spice powder.

Tamari — see Soy sauce

Toasted sesame oil
Made from white pressed and toasted sesame seeds, this oil is used as a flavoring/seasoning and is not suitable for use as a cooking oil since it burns easily. The flavor is intense, so use sparingly.

Tofu — see Fresh bean curd

Vermicelli rice noodle
Similar to vermicelli mung bean noodles, they come in many different widths and varieties. Before cooking, soak in hot water for 5 minutes. If using in salads, soak for 20 minutes. If using in a soup, add them dry.

Water chestnuts
The roots of an aquatic plant that grows in freshwater ponds, marshes, and lakes, and in slow-moving rivers and streams. Unpeeled, they resemble a chestnut in shape and coloring. They have a firm, crunchy texture.

Wheat flour noodles
Thin, white dried noodles. Do not confuse these with thick Japanese udon noodles.

Yellow bean sauce
Made from fermented yellow soybeans, dark brown sugar, and rice wine, this is a very popular flavoring ingredient in Sichuan and Hunan province in China. It also makes a great marinade for meats. Yellow bean paste is a thicker consistency, and is used in marinades, and as a flavoring in many savory dishes.

Zha cai (Sichuan vegetable)
A popular Sichuan pickled mustard vegetable used in hot and sour soups and dan dan noodles. The knobbly fist-sized stems are salted, pressed, dried, and then covered in hot chili paste and fermented in an earthenware jar. The taste is spicy, salty, and sour with a crunchy texture. Excess salt can be removed by soaking in fresh water. Usually sold in vacuum packs.

Index

Acknowledgments

I owe a big thank you to my publisher Joanna Copestick, my editorial director Judith Hannam, and Heather Holden Brown my literary agent and Kate Heather, my agent at RH Talent – without these four incredible women, *Wok On* would not have been born! Thank you so much for your belief and for your support for what I do. I am so lucky to have you all.

I must thank the incredibly talented and hardworking team I was so blessed to have! Thank you to editorial assistant Isabel Gonzalez-Prendergast and my copy editor Barbara Dixon for your attention to detail. Thank you to Caroline Clark for the fabulous cover design of the book and the funky illustrations. More than a few vintage bottles of champagne go to the incredible Tamin Jones for the photography, the hugely talented Aya Nishimura for the beautiful food styling, and of course the one and only Wei Tang for the props, as well as special thanks to Gemma John for the production of the book. This book really is a testament to your talents and would not have been made so beautiful without each and every one of you.

Biggest thanks and love to Chef Tom Kerridge for his amazing quote and support, as always. An idol and huge culinary hero of mine, I am indebted, and it means so much to have your support.

Thank you to Michael Kagan at ICM Talent and assistant Colin Burke in the US for continuing to support my career and for believing in me.

Thanks to all the powers at BBC, ITV, Food Network UK and US, Cooking Channel, NBC for continuing to give me opportunities and allowing me to share my cooking on the telly.

To all my family near or far, especially my mum and dad, thank you for all the sacrifices you made in order to give us a better life. I wouldn't be here without you and I am so proud of how far we have all come. This book is also for my three grandmas – Wu, Huang and Longhurst – thank you for your inspiration.

To Jamie, my husband, the vegan recipes I concocted for you are now in ink! Thank you for wokking with me through all that life throws at us, I can't imagine another wokker I would rather share my life with!

A huge thanks to all my fans – past and present – for continuing to support me on this culinary journey, this book is for you. I hope you are happy with the book and enjoy the recipes as much as I have in creating them. I am indebted and ever grateful for your love.

Writing a book isn't easy but I enjoy the process immensely and really this book is for all the cooks at home who have supported me time and again, over the years, it's you that I write the recipes for and I hope they give you as much joy as they do me, and that they sustain you and your family as your support has sustained me over these years.

I am truly grateful for this crazy journey...this girl that once grew up on a farm in southern Taiwan and ended up cooking on the telly in the UK, your support has made my dreams come true and not a day goes by that I don't pinch myself.

Thank you from my heart, for your love and kindness, this girl will continue to Wok On... and hopefully do you proud.